THE COLUMBIA QUIZ BOOK

JAMES RAIMES

COLUMBIA UNIVERSITY PRESS

NEW YORK

Columbia University Press
New York   Chichester, West Sussex

Copyright © 1993 James Raimes
All Rights reserved

Library of Congress Cataloging-in-Publication Data

Raimes, James
   The Columbia quiz book / James Raimes
   p. cm.
   ISBN 0–231–08079–4
   1. Questions and answers. I. Title.
   AG195.R26 1993
   031.02–dc20   93–17695
                                                  CIP

∞

Printed on permanent acid-free paper.

Printed in the United States of America

p 10 9 8 7 6 5 4 3 2

For Ann, Emily, and Lucy

CONTENTS

WHAT

WHEN

ACKNOWLEDGMENTS

Thanks to John Moore for his support and help. Thanks to Roy Thomas for his manuscript editing. And thanks to my colleagues who make Columbia University Press a good place to work.

INTRODUCTION

This general knowledge quiz book, drawn from the fifth edition of *The Columbia Encyclopedia*, has five sections (Who, What, When, Where, and How) devoted respectively to people, things, times, places, and numbers. If you want to take these divisions of knowledge more seriously, think of them as being devoted to Biography, the Material World (very broadly), History, Geography, and Measurement.

Each section has twenty sets of questions. Each set is on a different topic and has ten questions. So there are a hundred topics; and a thousand questions in all.

The first questions in each set on a topic are often easier than the last. And some sets of questions are easier than others.

You can test yourself systematically by reading through all the questions from the first to the last, referring to the answers at the back of the book when you need to. That way you will be answering ten related questions on one topic, then ten questions on another topic, and so on.

Or you can dip in here and there, testing yourself at random.

The answers usually tell you in a word or two whether you are right, then give you a little extra information on the subject.

If there are more than one of you on a car journey or sitting around the dinner table, you may want to test one another, in which case here is a suggested game for two people and a suggested game for three or more.

For Two People

A chooses a topic and is asked all ten questions by B.

Then B chooses a topic from a different section and is asked all ten questions by A.

If A answers five of the ten questions on a topic correctly, A chooses the topic next time A is tested. If A answers fewer than five questions on the first topic correctly, B chooses the topic the next time A is tested. The same goes for B.

Change sections every time you choose a topic. Score one point for a correct answer. The winner is the one with the most points after an agreed on number of sets has been answered by each person.

For Three or More People

A chooses a topic, and B asks A all ten questions.

If A answers five of the ten questions correctly, A chooses the topic next time A is tested.

Whenever A answers incorrectly, C must answer the same question. If C answers correctly, C gets two points. If C answers incorrectly, D must answer the same question and gets three points for a correct answer (and so on, continuing in a set order—for instance, clockwise). If all are incorrect, B supplies the answer. A continues answering questions, and when A answers incorrectly again, E (or whoever's turn it is) answers it—again for two points, if correct. When A has finished all ten questions, B chooses a topic from a different section, C asks B the questions, and so on. Change sections every time you choose a topic.

The questioner keeps the score at the end of each set and passes the score to the next questioner. The winner is the one with the most points after an agreed on number of sets has been answered by each member.

All sorts of variations can be played, and you can make up your own after deciding whether, for instance, you want to change questioners and answerers sooner than after every ten questions. A suggested scorecard follows this introduction.

NOTE

All the information in this book derives from *The Columbia Encyclopedia, Fifth Edition* (1993), although the key words in the questions do not necessarily correspond directly to the entry headings in the encyclopedia, and the words in the answers are not always identical to the language in the encyclopedia.

The Columbia Encyclopedia encompasses the world of knowledge from prehistory to the present day in fifty thousand entries. Each entry is a short essay offering good general descriptions of people, places, and things, and the reasons for their importance. The millions of facts in the encyclopedia have been thoroughly checked by academic specialists in more than a hundred fields from anthropology to zoology, and entries have been written to relate where appropriate to other entries so that you may pursue ideas from entry to entry. Bibliographies at the end of entries guide you to yet further information on subjects.

Ask at your local bookstore to see for yourself what a wealth of information is contained in *The Columbia Encyclopedia*, or order it directly from Houghton Mifflin Company, Order Processing, Wayside Road, Burlington, MA 01803. To order toll free, call 1-800-225-3362, or fax your order toll free to 1-800-634-7568.

PLAYERS & SCORES

TOPIC						
WHO:						
Biography total						
WHAT:						
Physical world total						
WHEN:						
History total						
WHERE:						
Geography total						
HOW:						
Measurement total						
GRAND TOTAL						

LOVERS

We are not dealing with Casanovas or Don Juans here, people remembered for the number and variety of their conquests. We remember the following people (real life and fictional) for the quality of their one great love.

1. Who (or, if you prefer, whom) did Mark Antony love?

2. Who did the Duke of Windsor love?

3. Who did Heathcliffe love?

4. Who did Troilus love?

5. Who did Dante love?

6. Who did Héloïse love?

7. Who did Lady Chatterley love?

8. Who did Jane Eyre love?

9. Who did Juliet love?

10. Who did Isolde love?

(Answers on pages 105-106)

KILLERS

*These people (real and fictional) have associated with them forever
an act which, however long planned, was over in seconds
and was momentous: they ended a life. In so doing, some of them
also changed the course of history.*

1. Who (whom) did Cain kill?

2. Who did John Wilkes Booth kill?

3. Who did Jack Ruby kill?

4. Who did Pat Garrett kill?

5. Who did Aaron Burr kill?

6. Who killed Goliath?

7. Who killed Marat?

8. Who killed Hemingway?

9. Who killed Hector?

10. Who killed Grendel?

(Answers on pages 106-107)

PARTNERS

In the following questions the names of the first five real-life or fictional individuals are usually (but not always) linked with those of their partners. The names of the last five couples, or pairs of people, have taken on such a special meaning that the name of either seems incomplete without that of the other.

1. Who is Spencer Tracy's most famous costar (they made nine films together)?

2. Who is Fred Astaire's most famous dancing partner?

3. Who is Sherlock Holmes's sober, credulous companion?

4. Who was Gertrude Stein's partner, the "author" of an autobiography which Stein in fact wrote?

5. Who was Don Quixote's partner in adventure?

6. Who is the doctor who takes a drug that transforms him into an ugly and horrific alter ego? And who is the alter ego?

7. Who wrote witty lyrics satirizing Victorian aesthetes, the navy, law, and women's education, and who was his musical partner who contributed to their partnership a wealth of melodic invention and orchestral ingenuity?

8. Who formed a research team in the field of human sexuality and established in St. Louis in 1970 a sex-therapy program that became a model for clinics elsewhere?

9. Who have minor roles in one of Shakespeare's tragedies but are the main characters (whose names are also included in the title) of a twentieth-century British play?

10. Who were the Italian anarchists found guilty in 1921 of killing a paymaster for a shoe company in Braintree, Massachusetts, and his guard?

(Answers on pages 107-108)

FAMOUS RELATIVES

The following famous people were each related, by blood or by marriage, to someone else who was equally well known. Some were related to more than one famous person.

1. Who was the female star of *Some Like It Hot* who also had two famous husbands? Name all three.

2. Who was the author of *The Turn of the Screw* and who was his brother?

3. Who was the composer of *Rhapsody in Blue* and who was his brother?

4. Who was the Russian pianist who made his American debut in 1928, and who was the Italian conductor who became his father-in-law in 1933?

5. Who was the female star of *Easter Parade* who had a famous daughter? Name both.

6. Name the actress who starred with her father in *On Golden Pond* (1981), and name at least two of her husbands.

7. Name the director of *La Grande Illusion* (1937) and his father.

8. Name the Mexican muralist who introduced a portrait of Lenin into a mural at Rockefeller Center in New York City, and name his wife.

9. Name the author of *Frankenstein*, her husband, and her mother.

10. Name the author of the syndicated column "My Day" (started in 1935) who was a U.S. delegate to the United Nations from 1945 to 1953 and again in 1961; name her uncle; and name the distant cousin whom she married.

(Answers on page 108)

PEOPLE WHO SAID SOMETHING FAMOUS

The following people summed up whole philosophies or encapsulated moments of history in language that could not be briefer or more simple. Some of them may or may not have said the words (their authenticity may have been challenged), but their names have become nonetheless irrevocably associated with the words.

1. Who said "L'etat, c'est moi"?

2. Who said "Let them eat cake"?

3. Who said "Cogito, ergo sum"?

4. Who said "Go West, young man"?

5. Who said "Give me liberty or give me death"?

6. What did Julius Caesar tell the Roman senate in 47 B.C. after defeating Pharnaces II?

7. What did Sir Henry Morton Stanley say on November 10, 1871, on Lake Tanganyika when he found the man he had long been searching for?

8. What was Nathan Hale reputed to have said on the gallows in 1776?

9. What did Archimedes shout when he jumped out of the bath and ran home naked in the third century B.C.?

10. What did Galileo say in 1633 at the end of the trial by the Inquisition, which forced him to recant his belief that the earth moved around the sun?

(Answers on page 109)

PEOPLE WHO GAVE THEIR NAME TO SOMETHING

The English language apparently does not have a word for a person whose name has become connected with a specific thing, nor for a thing which is called by the name of a person. However, these people and the things that are named for them are the subject of the following set of questions.

1. Who gave his name to a psychological test in which patients are asked to describe what they "see" in a set of ten standardized inkblots?

2. Who gave his name to a gas burner consisting essentially of a hollow tube which is fitted vertically around the flame and which has an opening at the base to admit air?

3. Who gave his name to a plan to foster economic recovery in certain European countries after World War II?

4. Who gave his name to a scale to measure earthquake magnitude?

5. Who gave his name to a map projection which has been more widely used for navigators' maps of the world than any other?

6. What did Johannes Wilhelm Geiger (1882–1945), the German scientist, give his name to?

7. What did James Van Allen, the American astrophysicist, give his name to?

8. What did Christian Doppler (1803–53), the Austrian scientist, give his name to?

9. What did Kurt Gödel (1906–78), the Austrian-born American mathematician, give his name to?

10. What did William of Occam (or Ockham; c.1285–1349), the English scholastic philosopher, give his name to?

(Answers on pages 110-111)

INVENTORS

Some inventions were not the achievement of one person but of several people; others were the brainchild of one person but were developed by someone else who got the credit. The following questions are concerned with the people who have been most associated with the invention's success.

1. Who invented bifocals?

2. Who invented the steam engine?

3. Who invented the telescope?

4. Who invented the phonograph?

5. Who invented the electric lamp?

6. What did Elisha Otis invent?

7. What did Cyrus McCormick invent?

8. What did Guglielmo Marconi invent?

9. What did Johann Gutenberg invent?

10. What did Eli Whitney invent?

(Answers on pages 111-112)

NOVELISTS

Good novels draw you into worlds different from your own so strongly that when you leave them, even temporarily, you can't wait to return. Great novels may transform you. Here are ten questions about the creators of these powerful narratives.

1. Who wrote *Pride and Prejudice*?

2. Who wrote *Crime and Punishment*?

3. Who wrote *War and Peace*?

4. Who wrote *Huckleberry Finn*?

5. Who wrote *Uncle Tom's Cabin*?

6. What novel by Ralph Ellison published in 1952 is considered a classic of American literature?

7. What novel did Flaubert write about the frustrations and love affairs of a romantic young woman married to a dull provincial doctor?

8. What novel by F. Scott Fitzgerald is the story of a bootleg-ger whose obsessive dream of wealth and lost love is destroyed by a corrupt reality?

9. What was Dickens's last novel, unfinished at his death?

10. What novel by Kate Chopin caused a storm of criticism because of its treatment of feminine sexuality?

(Answers on pages 112-113

COMPOSERS

Most works of classical music, however powerful, have uninteresting titles, such as Beethoven's Symphony no. 5 in C Minor (or the Fifth Symphony) or Rachmaninov's Second Piano Concerto. The works by the following composers are known by descriptive titles that go beyond their form number.

1. Who composed *Eine Kleine Nachtmusik?*

2. Who composed the *Brandenburg Concertos?*

3. Who composed *The Four Seasons?*

4. Who composed *The Nutcracker?*

5. Who composed the *Water Music?*

6. What work by Stravinsky was greeted with riotous disfavor by its first audience in 1913?

7. What is the collective title for Wagner's four operas based on a medieval Germanic epic?

8. What is the descriptive name for Beethoven's Third Symphony?

9. What is the title of Bizet's opera set in a world of Spanish gypsies and bullfighters?

10. What is the descriptive name for Schubert's Eighth Symphony?

(Answers on pages 113-114)

PAINTERS

Through created images fixed on a flat surface with a paint brush, the following artists or works of art have made millions of people see the world with new eyes.

1. Who painted the *Mona Lisa*?

2. Who painted a series of pictures of water lilies?

3. Who painted a series of pictures of soup cans?

4. Who painted *Les Demoiselles d'Avignon*?

5. Who painted the ceiling of the Sistine Chapel?

6. What is the title of the cubist-futurist painting by Marcel Duchamp that caused great controversy when it was exhibited at the New York Armory Show in 1913?

7. What is the title of Grant Wood's portrait of a stern rural couple?

8. What is the title of Andrew Wyeth's painting of a woman crawling in a field and looking toward a distant house?

9. What is the title of Salvador Dalí's painting with a watch hanging limply from the branch of a tree?

10. What is the actual title of Whistler's portrait of his mother sitting in a chair?

(Answers on pages 114-115)

MOVIE PEOPLE

Movies have proved to be by far the most alluring new creative form of the twentieth century. Here are ten questions about some of the people and films connected with this immensely popular medium.

1. Who directed and starred in *Citizen Kane* (1941)?

2. Who were the male and female stars in *Bringing Up Baby* (1938)?

3. Who directed *Rashomon* (1950)?

4. Who directed *The Seventh Seal* (1956)?

5. Who was the male lead in *Wuthering Heights* (1939), *Rebecca* (1940), and *Pride and Prejudice* (1940)?

6. What story did Francis Ford Coppola direct as a three-part sequence of movies, two of which received Academy Awards?

7. What classic American movie of 1942 stars Humphrey Bogart and Ingrid Bergman?

8. In what movie based on a Tolstoy novel did Greta Garbo play the title role in 1935?

9. In what 1966 movie (based on an Edward Albee play) did Richard Burton and Elizabeth Taylor star?

10. In which country did Charlie Chaplin settle in 1952?

(Answers on pages 115-116)

SPORTS FIGURES

These people inspired exhilaration and awe with their physical grace, competitive spirit, and, often, personal courage that extended far beyond the sports arena.

1. Who is "O. J." and what sport is connected with his name?

2. Who, outside of his sports achievements, is known for dying of amyotrophic lateral sclerosis?

3. Who defected from Czechoslovakia to the United States in 1975, and between 1978 and 1990 won the Wimbledon tournament nine times, the U.S. Open four times, the Australian Open three times, and the French Open twice?

4. Who regained the world heavyweight boxing crown by beating George Foreman in 1974, then lost it to Leon Spinks in 1978?

5. Who was the top NBA scorer in seven consecutive seasons (1959–65) and led the league in field goal percentage for nine seasons and in rebounds for eleven?

6. What team did Ted Williams play for from 1938 to 1960?

7. What gold medals did Jackie Joyner-Kersee win in the 1984 Olympics?

8. What event unrelated to basketball itself focused national attention on Magic Johnson in 1991?

9. What team was Wayne Gretzky traded to in 1988?

10. What country did Pelé play soccer for?

(Answers on pages 116-117)

GREAT THINKERS

These people thought deeply about knowledge, the mind, society, and the natural world. Luckily their thoughts have been preserved, so that not only their contemporaries but later generations could benefit from them.

1. Who wrote the *Republic*?

2. Who wrote the *Communist Manifesto*?

3. Who wrote *The Origin of Species*?

4. Who wrote *The Wealth of Nations*?

5. Who wrote *The Interpretation of Dreams*?

6. What is the title of Jean Jacques Rousseau's autobiographical work?

7. In what classic work does Niccolò Machiavelli describe the means by which a ruler may gain and maintain power?

8. Who studied under Plato and later tutored Alexander the Great?

9. Who studied philosophy under Bertrand Russell at Cambridge in 1912–13, served in the Austrian army in World War I, was an architect in Vienna, and returned to teach philosophy at Cambridge in 1929?

10. What was the life work of Denis Diderot, for which he enlisted the leading French talents of the time?

(Answers on pages 117-118)

SPIRITUAL LEADERS

These people led by the force of their example, which was peaceful, rather than by the force of weaponry. In doing so, they perhaps gained greater genuine loyalty in their lifetime than many warriors. In some cases the loyalty has lasted for centuries.

1. Who is traditionally credited with the authorship of the Torah?

2. Whose life was described, not long after his death, by a tax collector called Levi and also by a "beloved physician"?

3. Whose revelations are described in the Koran?

4. Whose sayings are collected in the *Analects?*

5. Who is traditionally considered the author of the *Tao Te Ching*?

6. What work contains the discourses of Buddha?

7. What national congress did Gandhi dominate from the early 1920s, enabling him to exact political concessions from the British by threats of "fasts unto death?"

8. In what country did Albert Schweitzer establish medical facilities in 1913 that received world financial support?

9. Against what city did Martin Luther King lead a 1955–56 boycott?

10. In what city did Mother Teresa start teaching school in 1927?

(Answers on pages 118-119)

MILITARY LEADERS

These people won battles. Most of them were successful enough to be honored by their countries, and some attained great political power.

1. Who was commander in chief of the Continental Army in the American Revolution?

2. Who was commander in chief of the Union Army in the American Civil War?

3. Who was general in chief of the Confederate armies in the American Civil War?

4. Who was supreme commander of the Allied Expeditionary Force in Europe in 1943?

5. Who was the American general in command of the allied invasion of Iraq in the 1991 Persian Gulf War?

6. What country did the "Desert Fox" fight for, and in what country did he win his famous nickname?

7. What city-state did Hannibal lead against Rome in 217 B.C.?

8. What country did Saladin fight against during the Third Crusade?

9. What country did Garibaldi fight to see unified in the 1860s?

10. What country was Gen. Douglas MacArthur in when he was recalled by President Truman?

(Answers on pages 119-120)

POLITICAL LEADERS

The people in the following questions used the political systems in their own countries to achieve great power, generally for the good of the countries concerned.

1. Who rallied and maintained British morale and resistance against Germany from 1940 to 1945, using stirring oratory, unceasing energy, and an adamant refusal to make peace until Adolf Hitler was crushed?

2. Who was the first popularly elected president in Russian history?

3. Who led the successful revolution against the corrupt Cuban dictatorship of Fulgencio Batista in 1959?

4. Who became leader of the national labor union Solidarity in Poland in 1980, was imprisoned in 1981, released in 1982, and awarded the Nobel Peace Prize in 1983?

5. Who was the leader of the parliamentary forces against King Charles I in the English Civil War?

6. In what country was Nelson Mandela imprisoned in 1964?

7. Of what country was Nehru the first prime minister?

8. What country did Ho Chi Minh lead against the Japanese, then against the French, and then lead part of against the United States?

9. In what country did a cardinal enjoy full control of the government from 1630 to 1642?

10. Of what country was the "Iron Chancellor" the premier from 1862 to 1890, and of what country was he chancellor from 1871 to 1890?

(Answers on pages 120-121)

CONQUERORS, EMPERORS, DICTATORS

These questions are about people who eventually died, as the rest of us will. However, before they did so, they imposed their will on such large areas of the world that their names still symbolize power and often fear.

1. Who was born on Corsica, conquered much of Europe in the early nineteenth century, was exiled to Elba, and later exiled again to Saint Helena?

2. Who was the illegitimate son of Maria Anna Schicklgruber, a servant, but went on to establish a twentieth-century dictatorship with a mission to achieve supremacy of the so-called Aryan race (which he termed the "master race")?

3. Who was born Joseph Dzhugashvili, headed a huge Communist state, and adopted repressive measures and terror tactics that reached their height in political purges of the 1930s?

4. Who was crowned "Emperor of the West" by the pope on Christmas Day 800?

5. Who conquered much of Asia between 1213 and 1224 to establish one of the greatest land empires the world has ever known?

6. Which people did Alexander the Great lead to conquer much of Asia in the fourth century B.C.?

7. Which people did Cyrus the Great lead in the fifth century B.C. to establish a vast empire stretching from the borders of Egypt on the west, possibly to the Peshawar region in the east?

8. Which people did Attila lead against the Eastern and Western Roman emperors in the fifth century?

9. Which people did Tamerlane lead to establish a fourteenth-century empire with Samarkand as its capital?

10. Which people was Montezuma ruling when Cortés seized him as a hostage in the early sixteenth century?

(Answers on pages 122-123)

LEGENDARY FIGURES

Most of the people in this category probably actually existed at one time. However, the incidents or exploits for which they are celebrated and remembered come not from the real world of history but from the world of legend.

1. Who was abandoned on a mountainside as a baby because an oracle warned that he was fated to kill his father?

2. Who was King Arthur's wife?

3. Who derived strength from his hair and pulled a temple down on himself and his enemies?

4. Who was the semilegendary chief of the Onondaga Native-Americans and founder of the Iroquois Confederacy?

5. Who was a Christian priest-king, monarch of a vast and wealthy empire in Asia or Africa?

6. What did the Pied Piper of Hamelin do?

7. What did Lady Godiva do?

8. What did Faust do?

9. What did William Tell do?

10. What did John Henry do?

(Answers on pages 123-124)

FICTIONAL CHARACTERS

Some fictional characters are so well conceived and portrayed that they live with us in our imaginations more vividly than their own creators. Name the following fictional characters or their creators.

1. Who is Shakespeare's Prince of Denmark who cannot make up his mind?

2. Who is Agatha Christie's egotistical Belgian detective?

3. Who is Bram Stoker's vampire?

4. Who is J. D. Salinger's schoolboy at odds with a "phoney" society?

5. Who is Dashiell Hammett's original tough-guy private eye?

6. Who created Falstaff?

7. Who created Snoopy?

8. Who created Pooh Bear?

9. Who created Scrooge?

10. Who created Peter Rabbit?

(Answers on pages 124-125)

GODS

This set of questions deals with figures who have been considered by humans to be typically greater than themselves—superior beings existing on some higher or supernatural plane (yet who nevertheless always seem to have some humanizing aspect that connects them to human affairs).

1. Who was the supreme god in ancient Greek religion?

2. Who was the primal goddess in ancient Greek religion, the mother and nourisher of all things?

3. Who was the god of war in ancient Roman religion?

4. Who is the supreme god of Hinduism?

5. Who was the supreme god of Germanic religion?

6. In what religion was Venus called Aphrodite?

7. In what religion was Huitzilopochtli the god of war?

8. In what religions was Ishtar the fertility goddess?

9. In what religion was Isis the nature goddess?

10. In what religion was Mithra the principal deity?

(Answers on pages 125-126)

ANIMALS

Humans are animals, and humans are diverse—but not in physical form or behavior as compared to the rest of the animal kingdom. These questions are about other animal species in the world.

1. What is the only mammal that can fly?

2. What animal reacts to an irritating object (such as a parasite or a grain of sand) in its soft tissue by producing a gem?

3. What animal has conspicuous black-and-white markings and defends itself by squirting an oily yellowish liquid with great force from vents under its tail?

4. What animal does the term *cuckold* come from and why?

5. What breed of dog was closely guarded for centuries by an imperial court?

6. From a part of which animal have such diverse items as piano and organ keys, billiard balls, and art objects been made?

7. What are the reproductive characteristics of the mule?

8. What were dinosaurs: reptiles, mammals, or amphibians?

9. What animal's skeleton is used as a product to retain water?

10. What are the only two mammals that lay eggs?

(Answers on pages 127-128)

PLANTS

Life on planet Earth is shared by those of us that can move around—we humans and the rest of the animal kingdom—and those of us that can't. These questions are about the latter.

1. What "forbidden fruit" did Eve give Adam to eat in the garden of Eden?

2. What is the fruit of an oak called?

3. What tree's wood is used extensively for piano keys?

4. What plant is grown commercially for the value of its fiber in making cordage but has also been grown for the value of the drug it yields?

5. What flower is a national emblem of Egypt and has been considered sacred since remote times?

6. Name the tree whose branch is a symbol of peace.

7. Name the tree, also called bay and sweet bay, which to the ancient Greeks symbolized victory and merit and was sacred to Apollo.

8. What plant was used in Egypt as a writing material from antiquity until the eighth century A.D.?

9. What edible fungi are traditionally hunted with dogs or hogs?

10. What do bladderwort, the pitcher plant, and sundew have in common?

(Answers on pages 128–129)

ELEMENTS, MINERALS, AND METALS

A very large part of our environment does not itself have life, although parts of it may have derived from living matter, parts may be present in living things, and parts may be essential ingredients of life.

1. What is the most abundant element on earth?

2. What is the most abundant element in the universe?

3. What chemical element forms more compounds than all the other elements combined?

4. What is the hardest natural substance known?

5. What reddish metal slowly forms a greenish surface film in moist air?

6. What metal is used in storage batteries, in plumbing, in paints, putty, and ceramics?

7. How many carats is pure gold?

8. What volcanic glass is formed by the solidification of lava that is permeated with gas bubbles?

9. What are the chief constituents of chalk?

10. What is the originating matter of coal?

(Answers on pages 129–130)

WEIRD BEASTS

Most (but not all) of the beasts in the following questions are mythical. The mythical ones often combine different parts of different animals, the fearsome products of fearful human imaginations. The weird beasts here that are not imaginary have a strange charm all their own.

1. What, in Greek mythology, was the sphinx?

2. What is the phoenix?

3. What is a coelacanth?

4. What is a unicorn?

5. What is a pterodactyl?

6. In medieval Jewish legend, what was an automaton-like servant made of clay and given life by means of a charm?

7. In Greek mythology, what was the offspring of Pasiphaë and a beautiful white bull?

8. In Greek mythology, what was a predatory monster with the head of a woman and the body, wings, and claws of a bird?

9. In ancient Middle Eastern legend, what was a creature with the head and wings of an eagle and the body of a lion?

10. What is a person who either willingly or unwillingly changes into a canine, eats human flesh or drinks human blood, then returns to his or her natural form?

(Answers on pages 130-131)

OUTER SPACE

These very distant, and generally very large, objects or occurrences are as surely parts of our environment as, say, the atoms in our bodies or the minerals in the center of the earth.

1. What are sunspots?

2. What is a white dwarf?

3. What is a red giant?

4. What is a black hole?

5. What is a quasar?

6. What is an immense body of highly rarefied gas and dust in the interstellar spaces of galaxies?

7. What does a comet's tail reveal about the direction of the comet's flight?

8. What are the bodies called that orbit the sun, are smaller than planets, and are generally irregularly shaped?

9. What are the small pieces of interplanetary matter called that fly through space and only become visible when they enter the earth's atmosphere?

10. What is an exploding star that suddenly increases its energy output as much as a billionfold and then slowly fades to less than its original brightness?

(Answers on pages 131-132)

UNIQUE THINGS

These things generally exist in only one form in one place. Here most of them are preceded by a particularizing name and by the definite article "the," both of which do the job of showing that they are unique.

1. What is the San Andreas Fault?

2. What is the Mason-Dixon Line?

3. What are the Elgin Marbles?

4. What is the Rosetta Stone?

5. What is Excalibur?

6. What is the name of the geological fault system of southwest Asia and east Africa that extends from north Syria to cenral Mozambique?

7. What is the name of the section of the Wall of the Haram in Jerusalem which is the only extant piece of the Temple of Solomon?

8. What is the collective name for the documents discovered in caves in 1947 which contain fragments of every book of the Hebrew Bible except Esther?

9. What is the name of the chalice (or cup or dish) identified in medieval Christian legend as the chalice of the Last Supper brought to England by St. Joseph of Arimathea?

10. What is the name of the throne that once stood in the audience hall of the Mogul palace in the Red Fort in Old Delhi?

(Answers on pages 132-133)

SCIENTIFIC INSTRUMENTS

Humans have designed a remarkable range of scientific instruments to extend their senses and abilities beyond the physical limitations of their bodies, and to make their lives easier. Here are some questions about a number of them.

1. What are thermometers for?

2. What are seismographs for?

3. What are barometers for?

4. What is radar for?

5. What are electrocardiographs for?.

6. What instrument in an automotive vehicle measures the total number of miles that have been traveled?

7. What is the instrument used for measuring the altitude of the sun or other celestial bodies?

8. What is the instrument used to determine the presence, direction, and strength of an electric current in a conductor?

9. What is the device used under water for locating submerged objects and for submarine communication by means of sound waves?

10. What is the electronic device used to produce visual displays corresponding to electrical signals?

(Answers on pages 133-134)

COMPOSITES

Some things look right, taste good, or work well when they are mixed with other things. Here are some questions about composites and what are generally accepted as their components.

1. What is ice cream generally made of?

2. What is brick generally made of?

3. What are the components of soil?

4. What is the "lead" in pencils actually made of?

5. What is gunpowder made from?

6. What is made from the hair of the Angora goat, either wholly or in combination with wool, silk, or cotton?

7. What is an alloy of copper and zinc?

8. What do you make by heating a mixture of limestone and clay until it almost fuses and then grinding it to a fine powder?

9. What is made from silica, an alkali, lime, and cullet?

10. What are you making if you brew and ferment cereals, especially malted barley, usually with the addition of hops as a flavoring agent?

(Answers on pages 134-135)

EVENTS

*These things happened or existed for a time in the history of the world.
Their importance was spectacular enough to earn them initial capital letters
in the history books.*

1. What was Watergate?

2. What was the Boston Tea Party?

3. What was the Battle of Britain?

4. What was the Underground Railroad?

5. What was the Vichy Government?

6. What was the name of the mass campaign from 1966 to
   1969 in China begun by Mao Zedong to revitalize the
   nation's revolutionary fervor?

7. What was the name of the unsuccessful invasion of Cuba in
   1961 by U.S.-backed Cuban exiles?

8. What was the name of the antiforeign movement in China
   in 1898–1900?

9. What was the name of the epic journey undertaken by
   China's communist Red Army in 1934–35?

10. What was the name of the wars undertaken by European
    Christians between the eleventh and thirteenth centuries to
    recover the Holy Land from the Muslims?

(Answers on pages 135–136)

INITIALS

Some things are much more easily remembered or said when they are reduced to the initial letters of their component words. Here are some examples.

1. What does CIA stand for?

2. What does IRS stand for?

3. What does IMF stand for?

4. What does UNESCO stand for?

5. What does AIDS stand for?

6. What does NOW stand for?

7. What does PLO stand for?

8. What does OPEC stand for?

9. What does SDI stand for?

10. What does AFL-CIO stand for?

(Answers on pages 136-137)

SPORTS AND GAMES

Humans spend a lot of time and money participating in healthy, generally physical competition with one another, either on their own or organized into teams. They spend even more time and money watching other humans doing so. Here are some questions about this basic human activity.

1. What sport has an annual Super Bowl championship game?

2. What game was said to have been created by Abner Doubleday in 1839?

3. What game centers around what happens to a vulcanized rubber disk one inch thick and three inches in diameter?

4. What sport has an annual international event at Indianapolis?

5. What game has a Ruy Lopez opening and a Sicilian defense?

6. Who originated basketball?

7. What country banned golf in 1457 and why?

8. Why is soccer so called?

9. Which countries contest for "the Ashes?"

10. Who originated the rules of modern boxing?

(Answers on pages 137-138)

TERMS AND IDEAS

You can't put your hands on these things, but they are (or were) quite real nonetheless. Without them, many intellectual notions, physical concepts, or social forces would be more difficult to grasp or understand.

1. What is the Oedipus Complex?

2. What was the New Deal?

3. What is habeas corpus?

4. What was Jim Crow?

5. What was Manifest Destiny?

6. What was the collective name for President Lyndon Johnson's vast domestic program of economic and social welfare legislation, first called for in May 1964?

7. What is the term used today to denote the Jewish communities living outside the Holy Land?

8. What was the name of the foreign policy first enunciated in a President's address to Congress on December 2, 1823?

9. What was the political slogan adopted by Irish nationalists in the nineteenth century?

10. What, in astronomy, is the systematic increase in the wavelength of all light received from a celestial object called?

(Answers on pages 138–139)

PROCESSES

The processes in the following questions take place inevitably in the natural world, or they are made to take place by humans for their own purposes.

1. What is metamorphosis (in zoology)?

2. What is syncopation (in music)?

3. What is grafting (in horticulture)?

4. What is osmosis (in chemistry)?

5. What is a filibuster (in legislative assemblies)?

6. Name the process by which green plants utilize the energy of sunlight to manufacture carbohydrates from carbon dioxide and water in the presence of chlorophyll.

7. Name the medical technique or treatment, based on traditional Chinese medicine, in which a number of very fine needles are inserted into the skin at specially designated points.

8. Name the process of skinning, preserving, and mounting vertebrate animals so that they appear lifelike.

9. What is the sum of all biochemical processes involved in life called?

10. Name the ritual act of driving out evil demons or spirits from places, persons, or things in which they are thought to dwell.

(Answers on pages 139–140)

CONDITIONS

The terms in the following questions describe conditions or states: states of nature, states of things, states of mind.

1. What is hibernation?

2. What is menopause?

3. What is symbiosis?

4. What is purgatory (in Roman Catholic teaching)?

5. What is REM sleep?

6. Name the deep state of unconsciousness from which a person cannot be aroused even with the most painful stimuli.

7. In economics, what is a persistent and relatively large increase in the general price level of goods and services?

8. Name the psychosis characterized by persistent delusions of persecution.

9. What, in Buddhism, Jainism, and Hinduism, is the state of supreme liberation and bliss?

10. In astronomy, what is the alignment of three bodies of the solar system along a straight or nearly straight line?

(Answers on pages 140-141)

FIELDS AND DISCIPLINES

These questions have to do with areas of study, or ways of organizing knowledge of the world. The terms themselves typically end in -ology or -ics and are appropriately derived from the Greek—the language of Plato's original Academy.

1. What is pediatrics?

2. What is semantics?

3. What is ethnology?

4. What is ethology?

5. What is ergonomics?

6. What is the study of the medical problems of the aged?

7. What is the study of the relationships of organisms to their physical environment and to one another?

8. What is the science of the life of past geologic periods based on fossil remains?

9. What branch of philosophy is directed toward theories of the origins, sources, and grounds of knowledge?

10. What branch of mathematics is concerned with those properties of geometric figures that are invariant under continuous transformations?

(Answers on pages 141-142)

DIFFERENCES

Some things may look alike or sound alike, but the differences between them are crucial. Mistaking one for the other can be embarrassing or costly. Here some examples.

1. What is the difference between arteries and veins?

2. What is the difference between bacteria and viruses?

3. What is the difference between etymology and entomology?

4. What is the difference between induction and deduction?

5. What is the difference between ontogeny and phylogeny?

6. What is the name of the female reproductive organ of a flowering plant, and the name of the male reproductive organ?

7. In limestone caves, what are the icicle-shaped masses of calcite attached to the ceiling called, and what are the cones of calcite rising from the floor?

8. What is the process of nuclear division in a living cell by which the number of chromosomes is reduced to half the original number? And what is the division in which the chromosome is exactly replicated and the two parts distributed to two identical daughter nuclei?

9. In ships or airplanes, what is the alternate movement of the sides up and down called; and what is the alternate movement of the front and back up and down?

10. What are the tough white cords of connective tissue in the body which generally attach muscle to bone, and what are those that generally join bones to other bones or to cartilage in the joint areas?

(Answers on pages 142-143)

PARTS OF THE BODY

Each of us is a complex machine with innumerable moving parts synchronized to perform innumerable functions. Even when we are doing "nothing," we can feel our chests moving and notice our noticing. How well do we know these parts of ourselves?

1. What are kidneys for?

2. What does the spleen do?

3. What is the diaphragm's role?

4. What is the purpose of the gall bladder?

5. What is the Achilles tendon?

6. What are the oviducts, or tubes extending from the uterus to the paired ovaries in the human female, called?

7. What is the glandular organ that secretes digestive enzymes and hormones, lying crosswise beneath the stomach in humans and connected to the small intestine at the duodenum?

8. What is the diaphragm that regulates the size of the pupil of the eye?

9. What is the technical name for the kneecap?

10. What is the gland that in males produces a thin, milky alkaline fluid into the urethra at the time of emission of semen?

(Answers on pages 143-144)

VEHICLES

The following conveyances, built to carry humans or other cargo from one place to another, did the job (or in some cases failed to do it) under such memorable circumstances that their names have come down to us through history as an essential part of the story.

1. What was the *Mayflower*?

2. What was the *Santa María*?

3. What was the *Titanic*?

4. What was *Apollo 11*?

5. What was the *Spirit of St. Louis*?

6. What was the name of the first artificial satellite?

7. What was the name of the U.S. space shuttle that exploded on January 28, 1986?

8. What was the name of the German airship that burned and exploded at its mast in 1937?

9. What was the name of the raft on which Norwegian ethnologist Thor Heyerdahl (b. 1914) crossed from Peru to the Tuamotu Islands in the South Pacific in 1947?

10. What was the name of the locomotive built by Peter Cooper (1791–1883), which first ran in 1830?

(Answers on pages 144–145)

FEATURES OF LANGUAGE

Language is one of the great achievements of the human species. It is an essential and ubiquitous feature of our environment, and almost invisible except when it is used badly or well. Here are some questions about notable features of language.

1. What is a metaphor?

2. What is a simile?

3. What is a paradox?

4. What is an epigram?

5. What is hyperbole?

6. What is the use of words, usually humorous, based on (a) the several meanings of one word, (b) a similarity of meaning between words that are pronounced the same, or (c) the difference in meanings between two words that are pronounced the same and spelled somewhat similarly?

7. What is, strictly, an inscription on a tomb; by extension, a statement, usually in verse, commemorating the dead?

8. What is the arrangement of words or lines in which a series of initial, final, or other corresponding letters, when taken together, stand in a set order to form a word, a phrase, the alphabet, or the like?

9. What is the figure of speech in which what is stated is not what is meant, but in which the user assumes that the listener understands the concealed meaning of the statement?

10. What is a word having a meaning that is the same as or very similar to the meaning of another word of the same language?

(Answers on pages 145–146)

NUTRITIONAL ELEMENTS

These questions are not so much about the fuel humans put into their bodies to continue functioning as about some of the special components of that fuel.

1. What is a calorie?

2. What is protein?

3. What is cholesterol?

4. What are carbohydrates?

5. What is the difference between saturated fats and unsaturated fats?

6. What are the five food groups?

7. What is fiber in food?

8. What chemical compound is: readily soluble in water but insoluble (or only slightly soluble) in most other liquids; an essential part of the diet of humans and animals; and a part of most animal fluids (such as blood, sweat, and tears)?

9. Which vitamin is ascorbic acid?

10. Which vitamin is carotene?

(Answers on pages 146-147)

HOLIDAYS

Societies around the world consider certain ideas or historical events or people so important that they must devote a whole day every year to their memory or celebration. In the following questions, the first six deal with special days in the United States.

1. When is Independence Day?

2. When is Veterans Day?

3. When is Labor Day?

4. When is Thanksgiving Day?

5. When is Martin Luther King, Jr. Day?

6. What holiday in late May was inaugurated in 1868 by Gen. John A. Logan and designated Decoration Day?

7. What Christian event is celebrated on December 25th?

8. What is the Hebrew name for the Day of Atonement which falls at the end of September or the beginning of October?

9. What is the name of the ninth month of the Muslim year, when Muslims must fast during daylight hours?

10. What is celebrated (but not honored) on April 1st?

(Answers on page 148)

SPORTS EVENTS

Almost every day on television and in the newspapers, the world of sports vies with all other news events for the attention of a huge audience. In popular culture exceptional sporting events not only stay in the memory, they practically become the stuff of legend.

1. When (in which year) did former heavyweight boxing champion Joe Louis regain his title by knocking out Max Schmeling?

2. When (in which year) did Billie Jean King defeat Bobbie Riggs?

3. When (in which year) did Jackie Robinson join the Brooklyn Dodgers?

4. When (in which year) did the Brooklyn Dodgers win the World Series of baseball?

5. When (in which years) did UCLA win a record-setting seven straight national basketball championships?

6. What African-American athlete won four Olympic gold medals in Berlin in 1936?

7. Who defeated Arnold Palmer in the U.S. Open in 1962?

8. What was the name of the infamous 1919 baseball scandal?

9. Who defeated Russian Boris Spassky for the world chess championship in 1972?

10. Who won four gold medals in swimming in the 1972 Olympic games?

(Answers on page 149)

HUMAN RIGHTS

Here are some questions about human rights (or, in a few cases, abuses) in American history. However progressive the United States may be in terms of human rights, we may nevertheless wonder at the relative lateness of the following dates in the history of the country.

1. When (in which decade) did women get the vote in the United States?

2. When (in which decade) was the *Brown v. The Board of Education* case decided by the Supreme Court?

3. When (in which decade) was the Bill of Rights ratified?

4. When (in which decade) was McCarthyism at its height?

5. When (in which decade) were the Salem witch trials?

6. In what 1973 decision did the Supreme Court rule, among other things, that states may not prohibit an abortion in the first six months of a pregnancy?

7. Who in 1955 refused to give up her seat to a white man on a bus in Montgomery, Alabama?

8. Who was tried in 1925 for teaching Darwin's theory of evolution against state law?

9. Where in 1848 was the first women's convention in the United States held?

10. Which amendment was added to the U.S. Constitution in 1865?

(Answers on page 150)

MOVIES

The first movie theaters, complete with luxurious accessories and a piano, were built in the first decade of the present century. They charged a nickel for admission and were called nickelodeons. Movies developed simultaneously as a new art form and as an industry. Movies now have a century of history, each decade having produced its excellent works. Ascribe a decade to each of the following.

1. When (in which decade) was *The Jazz Singer* first shown?

2. When (in which decade) was *Jaws* first shown?

3. When (in which decade) was *The Birds* first shown?

4. When (in which decade) was *The Gold Rush* first shown?

5. When (in which decade) was *Aguirre, the Wrath of God* first shown?

6. When (in which decade) was *The Treasure of the Sierra Madre* first shown?

7. When (in which decade) was *On the Waterfront* first shown?

8. When (in which decade) was *The Birth of a Nation* first shown?

9. When (in which decade) was *Top Hat* first shown?

10. When (in which decade) was *The Great Train Robbery* first shown?

(Answers on page 151)

EXACT DATES

Certain events in world history are so important and happened under such dramatic circumstances that we often remember the exact day, month, and year they occurred.

1. When was Pearl Harbor attacked?

2. When was John F. Kennedy assassinated?

3. When was D day?

4. When was the Bastille stormed?

5. When was Kristallnacht?

6. What happened on March 15, 44 B.C.?

7. What happened on August 6, 1945?

8. What happened on July 20, 1969?

9. What happened on May 28, 1953?

10. What happened on April 18, 1906?

(Answers on page 152)

CITY DISASTERS

Lucky is the city whose history does not include any terrible disasters. Cities are prone to them. Dense with buildings and people, cities can be devastated when fires or floods or earthquakes strike, or when they are attacked. In 1812, for instance, the British captured and sacked Washington, D.C., burning most of the public buildings, including the Capitol and the White House. The following questions focus on cities that have survived some kind of disaster.

1. When (in which year) was Kuwait attacked and plundered by Iraq?

2. When (in which year) was Dresden severely damaged by British and U.S. bombing?

3. When (in which year) was Phnom Penh captured by the Communist Khmer Rouge?

4. When (within a half century) was much of London destroyed by fire, giving Christopher Wren the opportunity to build many churches?

5. When (within a half century) did Rome burn, to be rebuilt by Nero?

6. Who sacked Troy around 1200 B.C.?

7. Who occupied Warsaw between 1939 and 1945 and subjected the city to systematic destruction?

8. What destroyed nearly half of Tokyo in 1923?

9. Who had been occupying Moscow in 1812 when almost the entire city burned down, except for the great stone churches and palaces?

10. Who sacked Baghdad in 1258?

(Answers on page 153)

BATTLES

The following occasions—of victory or defeat, depending on your point of view, but always of violence and presumably horror—have proved to be decisive turning points in the relations between countries or peoples.

1. When was the battle of Little Bighorn?
2. When was the battle of Yorktown?
3. When was the battle of the Alamo?
4. When was the battle of Gettysburg?
5. When was the battle of Dien Bien Phu?
6. Where did the Norman known as William the Conqueror defeat Harold of England in 1066?
7. Where did Henry V of England defeat an army of French knights in 1415?
8. Where was the Battle of the Bulge in 1944?
9. Where did Lord Wellington of England, Gebhard Von Blucher of Prussia, and Prince Schwarzenberg of Austria defeat Napoleon in 1815?
10. Where in North Africa did General Montgomery of England rout Rommel of Germany in October 1942?

(Answers on pages 153-154)

BOOKS

These questions are about works of nonfiction. In each case, one person sat applying words to paper day after day, articulating a view of one part of our world. Pages were filled, piled up, were read, printed, and today are read by thousands. Tell the dates of these works to within a decade.

1. When (in which decade) did Betty Friedan publish *The Feminine Mystique*?

2. When (in which decade) did James Watson publish *The Double Helix*?

3. When (in which decade) did Rachel Carson publish *Silent Spring*?

4. When (in which decade) did Virginia Woolf publish *A Room of One's Own*?

5. When (in which decade) did Simone de Beauvoir write *The Second Sex*?

6. Who wrote a famous diary on life in London in the 1660s?

7. Which French mayor of Bordeaux published a famous set of essays in the 1570s and 1580s?

8. Who wrote the *Life of Johnson*, published in 1791?

9. Name the eloquent account of near-solitary living in close harmony with nature published by Henry David Thoreau in 1854.

10. Name the work published by Alexis de Tocqueville in four volumes between 1835 and 1840.

(Answers on pages 154–155)

ART

Though they have achieved immortality, these works of art were labored over day by day by an artist. In the first five of the following questions, give the century in which this labor took place; in the last five, give the decade.

1. When (in which century) did Botticelli paint his *Birth of Venus?*

2. When (in which century) did Michelangelo sculpt his *David?*

3. When (in which century) did Goya etch his *Disasters of War?*

4. When (in which century) did Leonardo paint his *Last Supper?*

5. When (in which century) did Bruegel paint his *Country Wedding?*

6. When (in which decade) did Whistler paint his *Falling Rocket: Nocturne in Black and Gold?*

7. When (in which decade) did Rodin sculpt his *Thinker?*

8. When (in which decade) did Rousseau paint his *Sleeping Gypsy?*

9. When (in which decade) did Manet paint his *Le Déjeuner sur l'Herbe?*

10. When (in which decade) did Eakins paint his *The Gross Clinic?*

(Answers on page 156)

SCIENCE

Each of the following dates marks a major advancement of science, another step along the road toward clearer knowledge of our physical world. In the first five questions, give the centuries of the scientific achievement.

1. When (in which century) did Mendel carry out his genetic experiments?

2. When (in which century) did Mendeleev devise his Periodic Table?

3. When (in which century) did Halley observe the comet that bears his name?

4. When (in which century) did Hubble present his law?

5. When (in which century) did Newton publish his *Principia Mathematica*?

6. Who enunciated what is known as the uncertainty principle in quantum mechanics in the 1920s?

7. Who hypothesized the quantum theory in the 1900s?

8. Who developed a polio vaccine in the 1950s?

9. What theory did Maxwell summarize in the 1870s?

10. What did Rutherford explain in the 1910s on the basis of experiments carried out under his direction?

(Answers on pages 157–158)

WOMEN

These people are important figures not only in the history of women but in the history of humanity.

1. When (in which century) did Emily Dickinson live?

2. When (in which century) did Sappho live?

3. When (in which century) did Mary, Queen of Scots, live?

4. When (in which century) did Lucrezia Borgia live?

5. When (in which century) did George Sand live?

6. Who was czarina of Russia from 1762 to 1796?

7. Who was the first woman to make a solo flight across the Atlantic in 1932?

8. Who was "The Lady with the Lamp" in the late nineteenth and early twentieth centuries?

9. Who was queen of Bohemia and Hungary from 1740 to 1780?

10. Who wrote what is probably the world's first great novel in the early eleventh century?

(Answers on pages 158–159)

TECHNOLOGY

In human history, technological change began very slowly and for many centuries continued at a slow rate. With the Renaissance, however, the pace began to quicken. Now every year seems to bring something new. The following questions focus on certain technological inventions or improvements that changed the way humans lived their lives. In the first six, give the century of the technological innovation; in the last four, give the decade.

1. When (in which century) did windmills become familiar landmarks in Holland, England, France, and Germany?

2. When (in which century) were horseshoes first used?

3. When (in which century) were watches first made?

4. When (in which century) were canal locks developed?

5. When (in which century) was the microscope invented?

6. When (in which century) was the spinning jenny invented?

7. When (in which decade) was the revolver invented?

8. When (in which decade) was the first practical commercial typewriter marketed?

9. When (in which decade) was the fountain pen first successfully produced on a commercial scale?

10. When (in which decade) did the small all-purpose tractor come into general use?

(Answers on pages 159–160)

JOURNALISM AND THE MEDIA

These questions are about how people have communicated with as many like-minded people as possible about the important affairs of their day.

1. When (in which decade) was the first regularly scheduled radio broadcast?

2. When (in which decade) was the first transatlantic television broadcast?

3. When (in which decade) was *Ladies Home Journal* first published?

4. When (in which decade) was *Ebony* first published?

5. When (in which century) did journals of opinion, such as the *Review*, the *Examiner*, the *Tatler*, and the *Spectator*, begin to set a high standard of literary achievement?

6. What small-format monthly first offered condensations of books and magazine articles in the 1920s?

7. Which liberal opinion political journal, started in 1909, has had among its editors Walter Lippmann and Henry A. Wallace?

8. Which magazine, started in 1888, has been devoted to natural history, travel, and anthropological subjects?

9. What American newscaster became famous for his dramatic on-the-spot broadcasts from London during World War II?

10. Who was anchorman of the Columbia Broadcasting System's evening television news program from 1962 to 1981?

(Answers on pages 160-161)

ARCHITECTURE

People built the following structures with great skill according to a power-ful vision, one stone or brick at a time, usually over a long period of time.

1. When (in which century) was the Eiffel Tower in Paris built?

2. When (in which century) was the Parthenon in Athens built?

3. When (in which century) was the Colosseum in Rome built?

4. When (in which century) was the Taj Mahal in Agra, India, built?

5. When (in which century) was work on Notre Dame in Paris begun?

6. What was built in the thirteenth and fourteenth centuries overlooking Granada and became the finest example of Moorish architecture in Spain?

7. What was built in Cambodia in the twelfth century and became probably the largest religious structure in the world?

8. What masterpiece of Byzantine architecture, built in Constantinople (now Istanbul) in the sixth century as a Christian church, later became a mosque?

9. In which city did Antonio Gaudí begin his Church of the Sagrada Familia in 1882?

10. What city in the Puuc hills in the northern Yucatán peninsula of Mexico flourished between 600 and 900?

(Answers on pages 161-162)

STYLES AND MOVEMENTS

Strongly defined styles and movements in art and architecture usually have a descriptive label given either by the artists themselves or by their critics. But they flourished at a particular time. Surrealism in art and literature, for instance, was founded in Paris in 1920 and was at its height during the 1920s and 1930s.

1. When (in which half-century) did Impressionist painting flourish?
2. When (in which century) did Romanticism in literature flourish?
3. When (in which century) did Baroque sculpture and architecture flourish?
4. When (in which century) did Rococo painting and architecture flourish?
5. When (in which centuries) did Gothic art and architecture flourish?
6. What French art movement, begun in 1907, fragmented and redefined three-dimensional subjects from several points of view described simultaneously within a shallow plane, with a severely limited palette, rigidly geometric forms, and subtle and intricate compositions?
7. What art movement emerged in the late 1950s employing a common imagery found in comic strips and commercial art?
8. What art movement, emerging in New York City during the mid-1940s, was characterized by attention to surface texture and the glorification of the act of painting itself, and was the first important American movement to declare itself independent of European influence?
9. What British movement in art and poetry of the 1850s was founded by Dante Gabriel Rossetti, William Holman Hunt, and John Millais?
10. What decorative art movement—characterized by a richly ornamental, asymmetrical style of whiplash linearity, reminiscent of twining plant tendrils—lasted from the 1880s until the start of World War I?

(Answers on pages 162–163)

INDEPENDENCE

Each year in the following set of questions is the most important year in a particular country's history—the year it achieved independence from another country's domination.

1. When (in which year) did the United States become independent from England?

2. When (in which decade) did Mexico become independent from Spain?

3. When (in which decade) did Laos become independent from France?

4. When (in which decade) did the Republic of Ireland become independent from England?

5. When (in which decades) did the Baltic state of Latvia become independent from Russia and the former USSR?

6. From which country did Iceland become independent in 1944?

7. From which country did Brazil become independent in 1821?

8. From which country did Algeria become independent in 1962?

9. From which country did Zaire become independent in 1960?

10. From which country did Indonesia become independent in 1949?

(Answers on pages 163-164)

WARS

For many reasons, humans have organized themselves to fight other groups of humans in the world throughout the history of humanity. In some areas of the world they have done so for long periods of time. While the following wars all had various long-term causes (political or otherwise), history does record definite dates for their beginnings (usually, the outbreak of hostilities) and endings (usually, peace treaties).

1. When did the American Revolution begin and end?

2. When did the American Civil War begin and end?

3. When did World War 1 begin and end?

4. When did the Vietnam War begin and end?

5. When did the Korean War begin and end?

6. What war or revolution started in 1939 and ended in 1945?

7. What war or revolution lasted from 1789 to 1799?

8. What war or revolution started on June 5, 1967, and ended on June 10 of the same year?

9. What war or revolution proceeded in fits and starts, with one major phase in 1905, followed by two other phases in 1917, followed by civil war that finally ended in 1920?

10. What war or revolution lasted from 1936 to 1939?

(Answers on pages 164-165)

AGES AND ERAS

Some events or movements have so dominated history that they can be used to describe part of a century or even whole centuries. The Viking age, for instance, when Scandinavian warriors raided the coasts of Europe and the British Isles, lasted from the ninth to the eleventh centuries. Give the centuries that answer the following questions about other great movements or worldwide events.

1. When (in what centuries) was the Italian Renaissance?

2. When (in what centuries) was the colonization of North America?

3. When (in what century) was the Reformation?

4. When (what centuries) were the Middle Ages?

5. When (in what century) was the Enlightenment?

6. When (in what century) was the California gold rush?

7. When (in what century) was the Black Death?

8. When (in what centuries) was the Industrial Revolution in England?

9. When (in what century) was the age of Athenian democracy?

10. When (in what centuries) was the rise of Islam?

(Answers on pages 166-167)

EMPIRES

A prominent feature of human history has been the domination at different periods by one ethnic group of other (sometimes many other) ethnic groups. When the borders of these far-flung empires are superimposed on present-day maps, we see what feats of administrative skill or military organization they must have demanded. Today, at the very end of the twentieth century and the beginning of the twenty-first, it is just possible to speculate that the age of imperialism is over. Give the centuries of the following empires.

1. When was the greatest century of the British empire?

2. When was the great century of the Spanish empire?

3. When was France's Second Empire?

4. When were the greatest centuries of the Roman empire?

5. When was Byzantium's greatest period of splendor and power?

6. Which city was "Queen of the Seas" in the fifteenth century?

7. Which empire, within a century after the capture of Constantinople in 1453, was heir to the most ancient surviving empire of Europe?

8. Which European country's merchants traded in every continent in the seventeenth century, enjoying exclusive privileges in Japan?

9. Which European family established an empire in central Europe that reached its zenith in the early sixteenth century?

10. Which empire dominated southeast Asia from the ninth to the fifteenth centuries?

(Answers on pages 167–168)

HUMANITY AND PREHUMANITY

As we come to the end not just of a century but of a millennium, we may find ourselves thinking about what humans achieved in earlier millennia. If our millennium has been, among other things, the millennium of communication—by vehicles, by books, by television, by computer—what about earlier thousands of years? And then, what about those other chapters, all those millions of years, in the long story in which the history of humanity is a mere anecdote?

1. When (in which millennium) did humans first begin to write serious history?

2. When (in which millennium) did humans first begin to write?

3. When (in which millennium) did humans erect the stones of Stonehenge?

4. When (in which millennium) did humans paint the walls of caves near Lascaux, France ?

5. When (how many million years ago) did apes and hominids begin to develop along separate lines?

6. When (how many million years ago) did the dinosaurs become extinct?

7. When (how many million years ago) did cockroaches appear?

8. When (how many million years ago) were all fauna on our planet living in the sea?

9. When (how many million years ago) was the earth formed?

10. When (how many million years ago) was the universe formed?

(Answers on page 168)

CITIES

Cities constitute one of humanity's greatest collective experiments: in architectural design, in communal organization, and in political and social administration. Often beginning as a focal point for trade and commerce, they evolve into mass centers offering myriad attractions for visitors and inhabitants alike.

1. Where (in what city) is the oldest subway system in the world?
2. Where (in what city) were the 1972 Olympic summer games held?
3. Where (in what city) did Joseph Stalin, Winston Churchill, and Franklin Delano Roosevelt meet in 1945?
4. Where (in what city) did Harry Truman and Joseph Stalin and, later, Winston Churchill and Clement Attlee, meet in 1945?
5. Where (in what city) was the board game Monopoly invented?
6. Which densely populated city (or colony) will become part of China in 1997?
7. Which Australian city has a modernistic opera house?
8. Which European city has an international film festival each spring?
9. What was the city of the Medicis?
10. What city is at the eastern end of the Trans-Siberian railroad?

(Answers on pages 169–170)

CAPITALS

The following questions concern seats of government and the countries or states of which they are the capitals.

1. Where (what city) is the capital of California?

2. Where (what city) is the capital of Canada?

3. Where (what city) is the capital of Iraq?

4. Where (what city) is the capital of Vietnam?

5. Where (what city) is the capital of Lebanon?

6. Of what country is Bucharest the capital?

7. Of what state is Montgomery the capital?

8, Of what country is New Delhi the capital?

9. Of what country is Buenos Aires the capital?

10. Of what country is Damascus the capital?

(Answers on pages 170–171)

COUNTRIES

The places in the following questions are political units, with definite geographical boundaries and with various forms of self-government. But their interest lies in their innumerable differences rather than in their similarities.

1. Where (in what country) in South America is Portuguese the official language?

2. Where (in what country) is Tagalog spoken?

3. Where (in what country) was a 1,000-mile fence put up to prevent the spread of rabbits?

4. Where (in what country) were women first given the vote?

5. Where (in what country) did the Great Potato Famine devastate the population between 1847 and 1854?

6. Which country consists of many islands, the largest of which are Hokkaido, Honshu, Shikoku, and Kyushu?

7. Which country was named by Amerigo Vespucci after an Italian city?

8. Which is the world's smallest republic?

9. Which country is bordered on the north by Lebanon, on the east by Syria and Jordan, on the southwest by Egypt, and on the west by the Mediterranean Sea?

10. Which eleven states of the United States border Canada?

(Answers on pages 171-172)

CITY AREAS AND DISTRICTS

Within cities there are often smaller physical and social units famous for their distinctive flavor. These may once have been villages that were later absorbed into the larger entity of the city, or they may have uniquely developed within the already established entity. These neighborhoods or areas are the focus of the following questions.

1. Where (in which city) is Beverly Hills?

2. Where (in which city) is Beacon Hill?

3. Where (in which city) is Nob Hill?

4. Where (in which city) is Greenwich Village?

5. Where (in which city) is the Lido?

6. What is the area in Athens called where the Parthenon stands?

7. What is the area in Chicago called which is surrounded by a huge rectangle of elevated railroad lines?

8. What is the area in Paris called which is topped by the Church of the Sacré Coeur?

9. What is the area of Rome called where the pope lives?

10. What is the shopping and entertainment area in Tokyo called?

(Answers on pages 172-173)

STREETS AND BRIDGES

Many famous streets and bridges contribute a special look or feel to the cities they are in. An unforgettable sight in the very center of Avignon, France, for instance, is the fragment of a twelfth-century bridge that stretches only so far across the Rhone.

1. Where (in which city) is the Golden Gate Bridge?

2. Where (in which city) is the Ponte Vecchio?

3. Where (in which city) is the Bridge of Sighs?

4. Where (in which city) is the Great White Way?

5. Where (in which city) is the Reeperbahn?

6. What bridge links the boroughs of Brooklyn and Richmond (Staten Island) in New York City?

7. What is the name of the bridge that was dismantled and transported to Lake Havasu City, Arizona, where it was reassembled?

8. What is the name of the avenue connecting the Place de la Concorde in Paris with the Arc de Triomphe?

9. What street has been the center of English journalism?

10. On which elegant street in Berlin would you see the Kaiser Wilhelm Memorial Church?

(Answers on pages 173–174)

PARKS AND SQUARES

These places are often the most gracious parts of a city. Parks offer residents and visitors respite from the urban hubbub—a chance to relax and enjoy trees and grass, and perhaps flowers and birds. Both usually offer seats, and both offer the relief of open space.

1. Where (in which city) is Trafalgar Square?

2. Where (in which city) is Red Square?

3. Where (in which city) is Tien An Men Square?

4. Where (in which city) is St. Mark's Square?

5. Where (in which city) is the Tidal Basin?

6. What is the name of the amusement park in Copenhagen?

7. What is the name for the garden and park between the Louvre in Paris and the Jeu de Paume?

8. What is the park in Berlin that contains the Berlin zoo?

9. What is the name of the square in the heart of modern Prague?

10. What is the name of the olive grove and garden east of Jerusalem that was the scene of the agony and betrayal of Jesus?

(Answers on pages 174-175)

BUILDINGS

All the following are well known and well worth visiting for their architectural interest, or because of their historic or current significance.

1. Where (in which Italian city) is the world's most famous leaning tower?

2. Where (in which American city) is Independence Hall?

3. Where (in which city) is 10 Downing Street?

4. Where (in which city) is the Kremlin?

5. Where did William Randolph Hearst build a castle?

6. What is the largest office block in the world?

7. From which building in Dallas was President Kennedy shot?

8. What structure houses the crown jewels of England's royal family?

9. What structure did Frank Lloyd Wright design for Edgar Kaufmann in Bear Run, Pennsylvania, in 1936?

10. What ruined building near Chepstow in western England did Wordsworth write about?

(Answers on page 175)

INSTITUTIONS

The following questions deal with entities whose ongoing cultural, social, scientific, or other achievements bring pride to the cities that accommodate them. The Smithsonian in Washington is an institution of this sort.

1. Where (in what city) is the Louvre?

2. Where (in what city) is the Hermitage art museum?

3. Where (in what city) is the Prado?

4. Where (in what city) is the Tate Gallery?

5. Where (in what city) is the Uffizi Gallery?

6. What is the name of the famous psychiatric clinic in Topeka, Kansas?

7. What is the name of the great clinic in Rochester, Minnesota?

8. What is the name of the international organization concerned with the alleviation of human suffering and the promotion of public health, whose headquarters is in Geneva, Switzerland?

9. What is the name of the oceanographic institution in the town of Falmouth at the southwestern extremity of Cape Cod?

10. What is the name of the nuclear research center on the Franco-Swiss border west of Geneva, Switzerland?

(Answers on page 176)

BIRTH PLACES

Some people astound us by living lives of great achievement in countries quite different from those in which they were born. People of this sort are the subject of the following questions.

1. Where was Vladimir Nabokov born?

2. Where was Rupert Murdoch born?

3. Where was Maria Callas born?

4. Where was Salmon Rushdie born?

5. Where was Joseph Conrad born?

6. What American choreographer and ballet dancer was born in Russia in 1904?

7 What American cellist was born in France in 1955 and gave his first public recital in Paris at age six?

8. What British novelist was born in Iran in 1919 and brought up on a farm in Zimbabwe?

9. What painter born in Russia in 1887 spent most of his life in France, drawing subject matter from Jewish life and folklore?

10. What American writer born in Romania was awarded the Nobel Peace Prize in 1986?

(Answers on pages 176–177)

DEATH PLACES

These people died far from where most of their lives were spent.

1. Where did King Edward VIII (the Duke of Windsor) of Great Britain die?

2. Where did the Portuguese navigator Magellan die?

3. Where did the English explorer Captain James Cook die?

4. Where did the Scottish novelist Robert Louis Stevenson die?

5. Where did the American journalist John Reed die?

6. What American poet broadcast fascist propaganda from Italy during World War II and died in Italy in 1972?

7. What American poet, married to an English poet who later became poet laureate, committed suicide in England in 1963?

8. What witty Irish writer served a two-year prison term following a notorious trial and later died in France in 1900?

9. What Irish writer, whose novel using themes and images from Homer's *Odyssey* was charged with obscenity, died in Zurich in 1941?

10. What Welsh poet died in America of alcoholism in 1953?

(Answers on pages 177–178)

EVENTS

Some relatively obscure places have become well known in the world because of one particular event that happened there. The places in the following questions are of this sort. In the first five questions, name the event as well as the country or state where it happened.

1. Where is Guernica?

2. Where is Bhopal?

3. Where is Valdez?

4. Where is Lockerbie?

5. Where is Chernobyl?

6. What is the name of the sandy peninsula in North Carolina where the Wright brothers made their first successful airplane flights?

7. What city in the Netherlands was the site of the 1992 Treaty of European Union?

8. What site in New Mexico did the U.S. government choose for atomic research in 1942?

9. In what Bosnian city were the Archduke Francis Ferdinand and his wife assassinated in 1914?

10. In the jungle of what country did nine hundred self-exiled Americans commit mass suicide in 1978?

(Answers on page 179)

CHANGED NAMES

*Surely nothing is more important to the identity of a place than its name.
Yet the following places have had their names changed (sometimes more
than once) during their history. A few of these even remain better known by
their former names.*

1. What country used to be called Siam?

2. What country used to be called Northern Rhodesia?

3. What country used to be called Persia?

4. What country used to be called Ceylon?

5. What country used to be called Burma?

6. What was a former name for New York City?

7. What was a former name for Ho Chi Minh City?

8. What was a former name for San Francisco?

9. What were two former names for St. Petersburg?

10. What were two former names for Istanbul?

(Answers on pages 179–180)

PEOPLES

Many large ethnic groups—or sometimes social classes—in the world have (or have had) a rich tradition and dramatic history without having given their name to the countries in which they have lived.

1. Where (in which country) did the samurai live?

2. Where (in which country) did the Comanche live?

3. Where (in which country) did the Cossacks live?

4. Where (in which country) did the Inca live?

5. Where (in which country) did the Ashanti live?

6. Who are the two million people living in northeast Spain and southwest France, who have preserved their ancient, unique language?

7. Who are the roughly seven million people spread over Turkey, Iraq, Iran, and (in smaller numbers) in Syria and Armenia, who have been struggling, particularly in Iran and Iraq, for self-determination?

8. Who are the inhabitants (generally called Eskimos by Algonquian and European peoples) along the coast from the Bering Sea to Greenland and on the Chukchi Peninsula, in northeast Siberia?

9. Who are the roughly 30,000 people living in north Sweden, north Finland, and the Kola Peninsula of Russia, but concentrated mainly in north Norway?

10. Who are the roughly 225,000 indigenous people of New Zealand who speak a language related to Tahitian and Hawaiian?

(Answers on pages 180–181)

ISLANDS

Islands are the tops of otherwise submerged mountains, mountain ranges, or land masses. Many are uninhabited, but those referred to in the following questions are inhabited.

1. Where, in Upper New York Bay, did most immigrants enter the United States between 1892 and 1943?

2. Where was there a federal maximum security prison in San Francisco Bay between 1933 and 1963?

3. Where, west of Ecuador and on the equator, did Darwin find evidence to support his theory of natural selection?

4. Where did British troops fight an Argentinian force in 1982?

5. Where did the Minoan civilization flourish?

6. What is the largest island in the world?

7. What island off the north coast of France is dominated by a gigantic group of buildings, with an abbey church at the top?

8. Which island was mostly blown away by a terrific volcanic explosion in 1883?

9. What nation owns the Aleutian islands?

10. Which is the largest island in the Malagasy Republic?

(Answers on pages 181-182)

MOUNTAINS

Although mountains are the product of titanic forces exerted as plates move against one another in our planet's crust, they barely wrinkle the smoothness of the crust when seen from a distance. Here are some questions about these objects of beauty and awe.

1. Where (in which continent) is Mount Kilimanjaro?

2. Where (in which continent) are the Himalayas?

3. Where (in which country) is Mount Ararat?

4. Where (between which countries) are the Pyrenees?

5. Where (between which continents) is the Caucasus?

6. What volcano in Washington state erupted in 1980 after remaining dormant for 120 years?

7. What Japanese volcanic peak has inspired poets and artists for centuries?

8. What is the only active volcano on the European mainland?

9. What mountain was the mythical home of the ancient Greek gods?

10. Whose portraits are carved onto the face of Mount Rushmore?

(Answers on pages 182-183)

LAKES AND RIVERS

The following questions have to do with the stretches of water that are most intimately connected with land.

1. Where (in which continent) is the longest river in the world?

2. Where (between which continents) is the largest lake in the world?

3. Where (between which countries) is the largest freshwater lake in the world?

4. Where (between which countries) is the highest large lake in the world?

5. Where (in which continent) is the second-largest freshwater lake in the world?

6. Which river carries the most water in the world?

7. Which American river has given its name to a school of painting?

8. Which river starts in the Black Forest and ends in the Black Sea?

9. Which river flooded Florence in 1966?

10. Which country has the most lakes in the world?

(Answers on pages 183-184)

OCEANS, SEAS, AND GULFS

A very large part of the earth is covered with water or ice and much of it still remains a frontier for humanity. Most of the following questions deis part of the world.

1. Where (between which land areas) is the Gulf of California?

2. Where (between which countries) is the Adriatic Sea?

3. Where (between which countries) is the Yellow Sea?

4. Where (separating which land areas) is the Red Sea?

5. Where (in which ocean) are the Seychelles?

6. Which is the largest ocean?

7. Which sea was the center of the classical Greek world?

8. Which two bodies of water are joined by the Strait of Gibraltar?

9. What is the Bermuda Triangle?

10. Where is the Sea of Tranquility?

(Answers on pages 184–185)

AREAS OF THE WORLD

There are whole areas of the world that bear a name, but are not political units. The Maghreb, for instance, is the area of Morocco, Algeria, and Tunisia between the high ranges of the Atlas mountains and the Mediterranean Sea. The following questions are about other areas of this sort in the world.

1. Where (in what continent) is the Sahara?

2. Where (in what continent) is Siberia?

3. Where (in what country) is the Ruhr?

4. Where (in what three countries) is the Riviera?

5. Where is (what two countries make up) the Iberian Peninsula?

6. Name the three Low Countries.

7. Name the three Baltic States.

8. Name four of the five countries of Scandinavia.

9. Name four of the Balkan States.

10. Name the six New England states.

(Answers on pages 185-186)

THE EARTH, THE WORLD, AND THE CONTINENTS

This set of questions takes the long view. We are looking at our globe of earth in space, and at some of its constituent parts.

1. Where are the earth and the moon in relation to each other and to the sun during a lunar eclipse?

2. Where are the earth and the moon in relation to each other and to the sun during a solar eclipse?

3. Where is zero degrees latitude?

4. Where is zero degrees longitude?

5. Where (in which continent) is Guinea?

6. Nearest which continent is New Guinea?

7. In which continent is Guyana?

8. Is Venezuela in the northern or southern hemisphere?

9. Which is the smallest continent?

10. What is the difference between the land at the North Pole and the land at the South Pole?

(Answers on page 186)

FICTIONAL PLACES

Sorry, but you can't go to these places—except in your imagination.

1. Where was the legendary seat of King Arthur's court?

2. Where was the ideal state, founded entirely on reason, conceived of by Sir Thomas More?

3. Where was the legendary land of gold and plenty sought by the Spanish conquistadors in the New World from the mid-sixteenth century?

4. Where are the novels of *The Lord of the Rings* (1954–56) set?

5. Where did Gulliver go after Lilliput?

6. In Greek mythology, what is the name of the large island in the western sea, a place Plato described as a utopia destroyed by an earthquake?

7. In Norse mythology, what is the name of Odin's hall for slain heroes?

8. What is the name of the county where most of William Faulkner's novels are set?

9. What is the name of the county where Thomas Hardy set his novels?

10. What is the name of the county in the novels by Anthony Trollope about clerical life in rural England?

(Answers on page 187)

LENGTH

In some of the following cases, length is a conspicuous feature, as is the case with the Bayeux tapestry, the great embroidery chronicling the Norman conquest of England in 1066 by William the Conqueror. It measures only 20 inches from top to bottom but is 230 feet side to side (or end to end). With those measurements, it would be described as long, rather than wide.

1. How many feet are there in a mile?

2. How long (in feet) is the human intestine?

3. How long (in yards) is an American football field?

4. How many kilometers are there in a mile?

5. How far (in feet) can a human jump?

6. Which is the longer: an alligator or a crocodile?

7. Which is the longer: the distance a dolphin can jump or the distance a flying fish can "fly" out of water?

8. Which is the longer: a full-grown blue whale or a full-grown white shark?

9. Which is the longer: the longest snake or the longest worm?

10. Which is the longest: an African black rhino's horn, an African bull elephant's tusk, a walrus's tusk, or a boar's tusk?

(Answers on page 188)

HEIGHT

Termites are only about a half-inch long, but in their social groupings, which are almost organisms in themselves, they are able to build mounds up to forty feet high, a characteristic feature of the landscape in parts of Africa and Australia. If humans were to build residences proportionately large, the structures would be over a mile high.

1. How tall (in feet) is a giraffe?

2. How high (in feet) is a basketball hoop?

3. How high (in feet) can a human jump, unaided?

4. How high (in feet) can a human pole-vault?

5. How high (in feet) is Everest?

6. Which is the taller or higher: a full-grown California redwood or the Washington Monument?

7. Which is the higher: Angel Falls in Venezuela or Niagara Falls?

8. Which is the higher: the broadcasting tower in Toronto or the Sears Tower in Chicago?

9. Which is the higher: the ozone layer or the jet stream?

10. Which are the higher: cirrus clouds or stratus clouds?

(Answers on page 189)

DEPTH

The following questions focus on measurements taken from the outside in—toward the center or bottom of something (generally the earth).

1. How much of an iceberg, expressed as a fraction, is submerged?

2. How thick (in inches) is whale blubber?

3. How deep (in feet or miles) is the Grand Canyon, generally speaking?

4. How far (in miles) is it from the equator to the center of the earth?

5. How deep, or thick (in miles), are the continents?

6. Which is further below sea level: Death Valley or the surface of the Dead Sea?

7. Which is deeper: the depth at which scuba divers experience nitrogen narcosis or the depth sea lions can dive to?

8. Which are deeper: the burrows of badgers or the burrows of kingfishers?

9. Which is deeper: the lowest depth plants can grow in the sea or the depth sperm whales can dive to?

10. Which is deeper: the deepest part of the ocean or the deepest lake?

(Answers on page 190)

SPEED

Nervous impulses travel around our bodies at a speed of between 3 and 300 feet per second. Here are some questions about other speeds.

1. How fast (in minutes) can a human run a mile?

2. How fast (in miles per second) does light travel in a vacuum?

3. How fast is a knot?

4. How fast (in miles per hour or miles per second) must an object travel to escape from the earth's gravity?

5. How fast (in feet per second) does sound travel at zero degrees centigrade?

6. Which sprints faster: a thoroughbred horse galloping or a cheetah?

7. Which is faster: a roadrunner (the bird) running or a penguin swimming?

8. Which is faster: sap rising in a plant or a mole digging through soil?

9. Which is faster: the Gulf Stream or the solar wind (when it is near the earth and in a period of quiet sunspot activity)?

10. How many months does it take a human nail to grow from root to tip: one, two, or four?

(Answers on page 191)

FREQUENCY

Some things are so dependable, happening again and again at the same rate, that we build the smaller and larger schedules of our lives around them, as do other inhabitants of our planet. The following questions focus on this sort of regularity in the world or the universe.

1. How often are U.S. presidential elections held?

2. How often are Nobel Prizes awarded?

3. How often are the Olympic games held?

4. How often do leap years come around?

5. How often (beats per minute) does the adult human heart beat?

6. Which is the more frequent: a hummingbird's wingbeats or a bat's emission of sounds while flying?

7. Which is the more frequent: a "tommy gun" firing or the cycles of household electrical current in the United States?

8. Which is the more frequent: the earth and the moon's revolution about their common center of mass or the moon's rotation on its own axis?

9. Which is the more frequent: the earth's rotation on its axis or the sun's rotation on its axis?

10. Which is the more frequent: the earth's revolution about the sun or the sun's revolution about our own Milky Way galaxy?

(Answers on pages 192-193)

TEMPERATURE

*Here are some questions about one of the ways in which we can measure
our environment: by how hot or cold something is.*

1. How hot is water when it boils?

2. How do you convert a Fahrenheit temperature to Celsius?

3. How hot (above what temperature) are humans when they
   are considered to have a fever?

4. How cold is absolute zero?

5. How can you tell the temperature from a cricket's chirps?

6. Which is the hotter: the body temperature of birds or that of
   mammals?

7. Which is the hotter: the highest temperature on the surface
   of the earth or the highest temperature on the surface of the
   moon?

8. Which is the hotter: the melting point of iron or the temperature reached by the flame of an oxyacetylene torch?

9. Which is the hotter: the melting point of water or that of
   mercury?

10. Which is the hotter: the sun or the temperature at which
    fusion takes place to provide the energy for a hydrogen
    bomb?

(Answers on page 193)

WEIGHT

At Stonehenge one wonders how those stones, weighing up to one hundred tons each and each reaching sixty-five feet in length, were brought together from such great distances and erected to create a space of such awesome grandeur before 1500 B.C. Here are some questions about other weights.

1. How heavy (in pounds) is a human brain?

2. How heavy (in pounds) is a bowling ball?

3. How many pounds are there in a kilogram?

4. How much weight (in pounds) can a camel carry?

5. How heavy was the total assembly of Apollo moon spacecraft and launching rockets at each launch: 300 tons, 3,000 tons, or 30,000 tons?

6. Which is heavier: an ostrich egg or a human brain?

7. Which is heavier: an elephant or a hippopotamus?

8. Which would be heavier: a human brain or a brontosaurus brain?

9. Which would be heavier: a brontosaurus or a blue whale?

10. Which are heavier: the individual stones at Stonehenge or the megalithic stone heads on Easter Island?

(Answers on page 194)

DISTANCE

Here on earth you can think about distance in terms of miles or in terms of time—how long it takes to get from one place to another (usually hours or days, depending on whether you fly or drive). For cosmic journeys, as in the last two of the following questions, distance is more conveniently measured in terms of time.

1. How many miles are there in a marathon race?

2. How long (in miles) is a journey around the earth at the equator?

3. How far (in miles) is it from Washington to New York by air?

4. How far (in miles) is San Francisco from Los Angeles by air?

5. How far (in miles) is New York from Los Angeles by air?

6. How far (in miles) is North America from Asia at the Bering Strait?

7. How far is the earth from the moon: about 140,000 miles, about 240,000 miles, or about 340,000 miles?

8. How far is the earth from the sun: about 930,000 miles, about 9.3 million miles, or about 93 million miles?

9. A light-year—the distance light travels in a year—is about 6 million million miles. How long would a journey be to the nearest star (after the sun): .43 light-years, 4.3 light-years, or 43 light years?

10. How long would a journey be from the earth to the galaxy nearest our own Milky Way: 2,000 light-years, 200,000 light-years, or 2 million light-years?

(Answers on page 195)

AREA

Here are some questions about area. If you are not used to thinking in terms of acres or square miles, the first questions deal with yardstick areas, and their answers may help you think about the size of other areas. Before it was given a precise measurement, an acre was fairly easy for members of an agricultural society to imagine: it was the area that a yoke of oxen could plow in a day (and therefore differed in size from one locality to another).

1. How large is a football field: 5,000 square yards, 5,333 square yards, or 5,555 square yards?

2. How large (in square yards) is an acre?

3. How large are the White House grounds: 8 acres, 18 acres, or 28 acres?

4. How many acres are there in a square mile: 259 acres, 460 acres, or 640 acres?

5. How large is Central Park in New York City: 480 acres, 840 acres, or 1,480 acres?

6. Which is the larger in area: Manhattan Island in New York City or Grenada, the island in the West Indies?

7. Which is the larger in area: Texas or Spain?

8. Which is the larger in area: Iran or Iraq?

9. Which is the larger in area: the United States or Canada?

10. Which occupies more area on earth: sea or land?

(Answers on page 196)

NATURE

These questions are about the variety and teeming abundance of life around us.

1. How many legs does an insect have?

2. How many legs does a spider have?

3. How many arms does an octopus have?

4. How many legs does a centipede have (on average): a hundred, more than a hundred, or less than a hundred?

5. How many legs does a millipede have (on average): a thousand, more than a thousand, or less than a thousand?

6. Are there more bacteria or more insects in one gram of fertile soil?

7. Which are produced in the greater number: eggs (at the same time) by a crocodile or babies (at the same time) by a kangaroo?

8. Which is the greater number: eggs produced per day by a termite queen or eggs produced at one time by a common North Atlantic herring?

9. Are there more lions or tigers in their respective social groupings?

10. Which is the greater number: Mexican freetail bats living together in the Carlsbad Caverns of New Mexico or penguins in an Antarctic colony?

(Answers on pages 196–197)

THE UNIVERSE AND THE WORLD

Here are some basic questions about certain quantities in the universe and in the world. If the prospect of all the other humans in the world puts our own individual selves in perspective, some of the following numbers in turn put humanity in perspective.

1. How many states are there in the United States of America?

2. How many continents are there in the world?

3. How many planets are there in the solar system?

4. How many stars are there in our galaxy, the Milky Way: a million, a billion, or a hundred billion?

5. How many galaxies are there in the universe: under a billion or over a billion?

6. Where are there more hours of sunlight in the 24-hour period of midsummer's day: at the North Pole or at the equator?

7. Which exist in the greater quantity: chemical elements or languages?

8. Are there more species of fern or species of homo sapiens?

9. Are there more bird species or reptile species?

10. Are there more insect species or fish species?

(Answers on pages 197–198)

GROUPS AND GATHERINGS

When people gather together for a purpose, their numbers may be limited by rules, or they may not, in which case their numbers may be remarkably large. Here are some questions about groups of people in society.

1. How many people are there on an American football team?

2. How many people serve on a United States petty jury?

3. How many Justices of the Supreme Court of the United States are there?

4. How many United States Senators are there?

5. How many Joint Chiefs of Staff are there?

6. Which has more people: an American baseball team or an American basketball team?

7. Which has, or had, the greater capacity: the Colosseum in ancient Rome or the Astrodome in Houston?

8. Which is the larger number: that of runners in the New York City Marathon each year, or that of pilgrims to Mecca, in Saudi Arabia, in a year?

9. How many tenants does the Empire State Building accommodate: 2,500; 25,000; or 250,000?

10. What is the worldwide circulation of the *Reader's Digest*: nearer one million people, ten million people, or twenty million people?

(Answers on pages 198–199)

POPULATION

The following questions deal with how many people happen to live in certain places of varying sizes. As a basis for comparison, the present population (as of 1990) for Concord, Massachusetts, is 17,076, and for Yemen (as of 1991) is 10,050,000.

1. How many people live in Washington, D.C.: nearer one million people, two million people, or three million people?

2. How many people live in New York City: nearer five million people, seven million people, or ten million people?

3. How many people live in the United States: nearer 100 million people, 250 million people, or 500 million people?

4. How many people live in China: nearer half a billion people or a billion people?

5. How many people live in the world: nearer three billion people, five billion people, or seven billion people?

6. Which has the greater population: Alaska or Hawaii?

7. Which has the greater population: California or New York State?

8. Which has the greater population: the United States or Europe?

9. In the United States, which is the greater population: Native Americans, Spanish Americans, Asian Americans, or African Americans?

10. In the United States, which is the greater population: Jews or Muslims?

(Answers on pages 199–200)

THE HUMAN BODY

Our bodies show much symmetry: we have two hands, two feet, two eyes, two kidneys, and so on. But the two halves of the human body are certainly not identical (and the differences between men and women have not exactly gone unnoticed). However, the following questions generally apply to everyone and will test your knowledge about the fascinating complexity of our bodies.

1. How many milk teeth do we develop as children?

2. How many permanent teeth replace our milk teeth at about age six?

3. How many quarts of blood does an average adult male have in his body?.

4. How many bones do we have in our body: nearer one hundred, five hundred, or a thousand?

5. How many chromosomes do humans have in every cell of their bodies?

6. Which has more bones—the hand or the foot?

7. Which are the more numerous: immature eggs in the cortex of a female infant's ovary at birth or mature eggs released every twenty-eight days during puberty?

8. Which are the more numerous: salivary glands or fundamental tastes that can be tasted?

9. Which are more numerous: chambers in the heart or types of muscle?

10. Which contains the most water: muscle tissue or red blood cells?

(Answers on pages 200–201)

PERIODS OF POWER

*The following questions focus on how long certain people held power—
which may be of greater significance, for history and for the people they
ruled, than how long they lived.*

1. How long was John Kennedy president of the United
   States: nearer two years, three years, or four years (one
   term)?

2. How long was Lincoln president of the United States: less
   than one term or more than one term?

3. How long was Margaret Thatcher prime minister of Great
   Britain: four years, eight years, or twelve years.?

4. How long was the reign of Queen Elizabeth I of England:
   less than twenty-five years or more than twenty-five years?

5. How long was Louis XIV king of France: more than seventy
   years or less than seventy years?

6. Who held power in the People's Republic of China for
   twenty-seven years—from 1949 to 1976?

7. Who ruled Iran for ten years starting in 1979?

8. Who was prime minister of Israel for the five years from
   1969 to 1974?

9. Who was the first Roman emperor (for forty-three years,
   from 29 B.C. until A.D. 14), a grand-nephew and heir of
   Julius Caesar?

10. Who was the first tsar of Russia for thirty-seven years, from
    1547 until 1584 (and the subject of a famous film by the
    master Russian director, Sergei Eisenstein)?

(Answers on pages 201-202)

NUMBERS IN RELIGION AND MYTHOLOGY

The main religions of the ancient and the modern worlds have had or have certain numbers that feature importantly in their belief system. Here are some questions dealing with this particular aspect of religion and mythology.

1. How many commandments were given by God to Moses?

2. How many Persons of God are there in Christianity?

3. How many disciples did Jesus have?

4. How many branches does the menorah have?

5. How many Fates were there in ancient Greek mythology/religion?

6. What are the Four Stages of Hindu life?

7. Who are the nine Muses of ancient Greek mythology/religion?

8. What are the Five Duties in Islam?

9. What are the Eight Paths in Buddhism?

10. What are the Five Relations in Confucianism?

(Answers on pages 202-203)

DEATH TOLLS

Death is the one inevitable fact in the general landscape of life, yet some deaths or killings are particularly horrific to us because of their large numbers or terrible circumstances. Here are some unsettling questions on a grim subject.

1. How many Jews were killed in the Holocaust?
2. How many people were killed at My Lai in 1968?
3. How many people were killed when U.S. atom bombs were dropped on the Japanese cities of Hiroshima and Nagasaki in August 1945?
4. How many people were killed in the Battle of Antietam during the American Civil War?
5. How many were killed in the American Civil War?
6. Which was the greater number: those British killed in the third Battle of Ypres (also known as Passchendaele) in World War I, or Allied casualties at the Battle of the Bulge (also known as the Battle of the Ardennes) in World War II?
7. Which killed more people: World War I or the influenza epidemic after it?
8. Which killed more Americans: the Korean War or the Vietnam War?
9. Which was the greater number: the burnings at the stake in the last three years of "Bloody Mary's" reign, or the number of Jews who died in the Warsaw ghetto under German occupation in World War II?
10. Which was the greater number: the crucifixions after Spartacus's slave revolt at Capua in 71 B.C., or the number of suicides when the Romans took Masada in A.D. 73?

(Answers on pages 203-205)

AGE AND ACHIEVEMENT

When people achieve something remarkable at an early age, we may be thrilled and at the same time experience a sense of envy and loss. When they achieve something remarkable at a great age, we may feel there is hope for us yet. The people in the following questions are of each sort.

1. How old was Kennedy when he was elected president: in his thirties, forties, or fifties?

2. How old was Keats when he died: in his teens, twenties, or thirties?

3. How old was Anne Frank when she died in a Nazi concentration camp: in her teens, twenties, or thirties?

4. How old was Picasso when he painted *The Old Guitarist*: in his twenties, sixties, or nineties?

5. How old was Einstein when he formulated the special theory of relativity: in his twenties, fifties, or seventies?

6. What businessman founded the computer software company Microsoft Inc. at the age of nineteen?

7. Which painter made brilliantly colorful cutouts and stencils, such as *Jazz*, at age seventy-eight?

8. Who became president at age forty-two when William McKinley was assassinated?

9. Which philosopher was imprisoned at age seventy-nine for activity in mass demonstrations to ban nuclear weapons in 1961?

10. Who was awarded the Nobel Prize for physiology or medicine in 1983 at age eighty-one?

(Answers on page 205-206)

HOW THEY DIED

These people were executed or assassinated, most of them because they were considered threatening to the people in power at the time. The following questions focus on how (by what means or method) they actually were killed.

1. How was Jesus executed?

2. How was Socrates executed?

3. How was Joan of Arc executed?

4. How was Charles I of England, Scotland, and Ireland executed?

5. How was Louis XVI of France executed?

6. Who died as a result of mistreatment in South African police custody in 1977, having founded an organization for black students and developed a national "black consciousness" movement?

7. Who was shot in 1968 just after having won the California Democratic primary?

8. Who was beheaded in 1536 after having borne King Henry VIII of England a daughter and having been convicted of adultery and incest?

9. Who was stabbed to death while trying to escape from prison in 1877, a year after helping defeat Custer at Little Bighorn?

10. Who was hanged in 1831 after he had led the Southampton Insurrection in Virginia?

(Answers on pages 206–207)

MONEY-MAKERS

Some people's names were connected with money long before they were connected with philanthropy or anything else. The Rockefeller fortune, which has benefited countless people besides the Rockefeller family, was built up by John D. Rockefeller (1839–1937), who in his lifetime dominated the oil-refining industry. The following people also made enough money to allow their names to be connected to something quite different.

1. How did Alfred Nobel make his money?

2. How was the Onassis fortune made?

3. How was the Kennedy money made?

4. How did the Medicis make their money?

5. How did Andrew Carnegie make his money?

6. Who started as a boy ferrying freight between Staten Island and Manhattan, came to dominate the regional ferry business, then went into the railroad business, in which he amassed a fortune?

7. In 1822 Emperor Francis I of Austria made five brothers barons. They were bankers, each in a different city: Frankfurt, Vienna, London, Naples, and Paris. Who were they?

8. Who wrested control of the Albany and Susquehanna Railroad from Jay Gould and Jim Fisk in 1869 and developed a railroad empire by reorganizations and consolidations in all parts of the United States?

9. Who, as the acting head of the Carnegie Steel Company, took an adamant antiunion stand that led to a pitched battle in the 1892 strike at Homestead, Pennsylvania?

10. Who in 1987 was paid $550 million by his company, Drexel Burnham Lambert, Inc?

(Answers on pages 207–208)

WHO

LOVERS

1. Cleopatra. The Egyptian queen (69–30 B.C.) was one of the great romantic heroines of all time. Before Mark Antony, she had been the lover of Julius Caesar.
2. Wallis Warfield Simpson (1896-1936). The American woman's projected marriage to King Edward VIII of Great Britain after her second divorce precipitated Edward's abdication from the throne in 1936.
3. Catherine Earnshaw. The wild, passionate story of the intense, almost demonic love between Heathcliffe and Catherine is the subject of Emily Brontë's masterpiece *Wuthering Heights* (1847).
4. Cressida, in Shakespeare's version (1601) of the legend. In Chaucer's version, she was Criseyde. The term "pander" comes from Pandarus, who procured Cressida for Troilus.
5. Beatrice. Dante first saw Beatrice Portinari when he was nine years old, and she remained his ideal and inspiration until his death. She is believed to be the Beatrice of the *Divine Comedy* and of the *Vita Nuova*.
6. Peter Abelard. The French philosopher and teacher (1079–1142) is regarded as the founder of the University of Paris. The events of his life, including his love for Héloïse and his castration by thugs hired by her uncle, are revealed in their poignant letters to each other.
7. Her husband's gamekeeper (Mellors). D. H. Lawrence's novel, *Lady Chatterley's Lover* (1928), was banned in England and the United States for many years because of its explicit descriptions of sexual lovemaking in intimate detail.
8. Mr. Rochester. Jane Eyre is a governess employed by the Byronic Mr. Rochester in Charlotte Brontë's great novel *Jane Eyre* (1847).

9. Romeo. Shakespeare's tragedy of young love was written about 1594. The Broadway musical *West Side Story* (1957, filmed 1961) is a popular recent version of the story.

10. Tristan (Tristram). There are many versions of this medieval romance, including one in Arthurian legend. Modern versions include Richard Wagner's opera *Tristan und Isolde* (1857–59).

KILLERS

1. Abel. In the Bible, Cain was the eldest son of Adam and Eve and was a "tiller of the soil."

2. Abraham Lincoln (1809–65). Booth (1838–65), a star Shakespearian actor and ardent Confederate sympathizer, shot President Lincoln on April 14, 1865, at Ford's Theater in Washington, D.C.

3. Lee Harvey Oswald (1939–63). Oswald was the presumed assassin of President John F. Kennedy. Two days after the assassination in Dallas, Texas, Ruby, a nightclub proprietor, shot Oswald while he was in police hands.

4. Billy the Kid (1859–81). The American outlaw, whose real name was William H. Bonney, had killed several men before he was sixteen years old. He led a cattle-rustling gang, killed a sheriff, was captured and sentenced to death, escaped, but was trapped and shot by Sheriff Patrick Floyd "Pat" Garrett.

5. Alexander Hamilton (1755–1804). Burr, the American political leader (1756–1836), killed Hamilton, a noted Federalist and one of the founding fathers of the United States, in a duel at Weehawken Heights, New Jersey, in 1804.

6. David. In the Bible he killed the gigantic Philistine with a slingshot. David was later chosen king of the Hebrews (d. c. 972 B.C.).

7. Charlotte Corday (1768–93). Corday, who was emulating Brutus, one of Julius Caesar's assassins, stabbed Jean Paul Marat (1743–93), the French revolutionary leader, to death in his bath. She was guillotined.

8. Ernest Hemingway (1899–1961) shot himself.

9. Achilles. The Greek mythological hero killed the Trojan hero Hector in revenge for the death of Patroclus.

10. Beowulf. *Beowulf* is the oldest extant English epic (a text written c. A.D. 1000 exists). In it the hero kills the water monster Grendel.

PARTNERS

1. Katharine Hepburn. Spencer Tracy (1900–67) and Katharine Hepburn (b. 1907) made a partnership full of humor and intelligence.

2. Ginger Rogers. Fred Astaire (1899–1987) and Ginger Rogers (b. 1911) made popular dance into an elegant, disciplined art form.

3. Dr. Watson. Holmes and Watson, appearing together in many books (and films, teleplays, etc.), are the creations of Sir Arthur Conan Doyle (1859–1930).

4. Alice B. Toklas. Gertrude Stein (1874–946) actually wrote *The Autobiography of Alice B. Toklas* (1933) about herself.

5. Sancho Panza. The adventures of Don Quixote and Sancho Panza are related by Miguel de Cervantes (1547–616) in *Don Quixote*, an unforgettable description of the transforming power of illusion.

6. Dr. Jekyll and Mr. Hyde. In his great moral science fiction thriller, which bears their names, Robert Louis Stevenson (1850–94) created a modern-day monster who lives two existences—one good, one evil.

7. Gilbert and Sullivan. Sir William Gilbert (1836–1911) was the lyricist, and Sir Arthur Sullivan (1842–1900) was the composer. Their operettas were so successful that Richard D'Oyly Carte built the Savoy Theatre expressly for their production.

8. Masters and Johnson. William H. Masters (b. 1915) and Virginia E. Johnson (b. 1925), published *Human Sexual Response* (1966) and other works. Masters and Johnson were married from 1971 to 1992.

9. Rosenkrantz and Guildenstern. Minor characters in *Hamlet*, they are moved to center stage in British playwright Tom Stoppard's *Rosenkrantz and Guildenstern Are Dead* (1966), the comic play that brought him to prominence.

10. Sacco and Vanzetti. Many people believed that the conviction of Nicola Sacco and Bartolomeo Vanzetti was unwarranted and had been unduly influenced by their reputation as anarchists at a time when antiradical sentiment was running high.

FAMOUS RELATIVES

1. Marilyn Monroe (1926–62); Joe DiMaggio (b. 1914), the baseball player; and Arthur Miller (b. 1915), the playwright.
2. Henry James (1843–82) and William James (1842–1910), the American philosopher of pragmatism and radical empiricism.
3. George Gershwin (1898–1937) and his brother Ira Gershwin (1896–1983), who wrote the lyrics to many of George's songs.
4. Vladimir Horowitz (1904–91) and Arturo Toscanini (1867–1957). Horowitz was one of the world's most popular virtuoso pianists, and Toscanini was one of the world's great conductors.
5. Judy Garland (1922–69) and her daughter, singer-actress Liza Minnelli (b. 1946), an Oscar winner for *Cabaret* (1972).
6. Jane Fonda (b. 1937); her father Henry Fonda (1905–1982), and her husbands French film director Roger Vadim, Sixties political activist Tom Hayden, and media mogul Ted Turner.
7. Jean Renoir (1894–1979) and his father Pierre-Auguste Renoir (1841–1919), the French impressionist painter and sculptor.
8. Diego Rivera (1886–1957) and his wife Frida Kahlo (1907–54), the Mexican painters. The controversial mural in New York City was destroyed because of Lenin's inclusion, but was later reproduced in Mexico City.
9. Mary Wollstonecraft Shelley (1797–1851) was married to Percy Bysshe Shelley (1792–1822), the English poet. Her mother was Mary Wollstonecraft (1759–97), the author of the first great document of feminism, *Vindication of the Rights of Women* (1792).
10. Eleanor Roosevelt (1884–1962); her uncle Theodore Roosevelt (1858–1919), twenty-sixth president of the United States; and Franklin Delano Roosevelt (1882–1945), thirty-second president of the United States).

PEOPLE WHO SAID SOMETHING FAMOUS

1. Louis XIV (1638–1715). His reign, an absolute monarchy based on divine right, can be characterized by these words ("I am the state") attributed to him.
2. Marie Antoinette (1755–93). This queen of France, guillotined during the French Revolution, was said to have proposed this as a solution to the bread famine in France.
3. René Descartes (1596–1650). These words, "I think, therefore I am," are the kernel of his philosophy, which begins with universal skepticism: there is one thing that cannot be doubted—doubt itself.
4. Horace Greeley (1811–72). Thousands of Americans heeded the advice to "Go West," said to have been given by Greeley, editor and founder of the New York *Tribune* (1841).
5. Patrick Henry (1736–99). Henry was a political leader in the American Revolution, and a great orator. He also said, "If this be treason, make the most of it."
6. "I came, I saw, I conquered." Caesar (102?–44 B.C.) was at the height of his military and political power when he defeated Pharnaces at Pontus in 47 B.C. and said "Veni, vidi, vici."
7. "Dr. Livingstone, I presume?" Stanley (1841–904), the American journalist and empire builder, had been sent by the New York *Herald* to Africa to find the explorer David Livingstone.
8. "I only regret that I have but one life to lose for my country." In the American Revolution, Hale (1755–76) volunteered to get information about the British forces on Long Island. He disguised himself as a schoolmaster, was discovered, captured, and hanged without trial.
9. "Eureka! Eureka!" ("I have found it! I have found it!"). The ruler Hiero II of Syracuse had asked Archimedes to find a method of determining whether a crown was pure gold or alloyed with silver. As he stepped into his bath, Archimedes realized that a given weight of gold would displace less water than an equal weight of silver (which is less dense than gold).
10. "Yet it does move." As he rose from his knees, Galileo Galilei (1564–1642) is reputed to have whispered, "E pur si muove."

PEOPLE WHO GAVE THEIR NAME TO SOMETHING

1. Hermann Rorschach (1884–1922), the Swiss psychiatrist. The interpretation of the results of a Rorschach test is based on whether the whole blot or details are described, the reaction to color, how much movement is seen, and a great many other factors.

2. Robert Bunsen (1811–99). The German scientist made many important scientific discoveries and invented several kinds of laboratory equipment. His Bunsen burner produces a smokeless, nonluminous flame of high temperature.

3. George C. Marshall (1880–1959). Marshall was U.S. Secretary of State from 1947 to 1949. For his Marshall Plan he received the 1953 Nobel Peace Prize.

4. Charles F. Richter (1900–85). The American seismologist devised the Richter scale in 1935. Scale numbers range from 0 to 9. Earthquakes greater than about 4.5 on this scale can cause damage. Those greater than 7 are severe.

5. Gerardus Mercator (1512–94), the Flemish cartographer. Projections transfer the features of the surface of the earth (or other spherical object) onto a flat surface—with some inevitable loss of accuracy. In the Mercator projection, the size of Greenland is enormously exaggerated.

6. A portable radiation counter. The German scientist participated with A. Muller in the 1928 improvement of the Geiger Counter first developed by Hans Geiger.

7. A belt of radiation above the earth. Van Allen was the first to interpret the findings of the Explorer I satellite in 1958. The Van Allen radiation belt lies between 400 and 40,000 miles above the earth.

8. A physical effect visible or audible when a wavelength of energy in the form of light waves or sound waves changes as the source or the receiver moves. The Doppler Effect is illustrated by the pitch of a train whistle suddenly dropping as it passes a stationary listener.

9. A theorem stating that the various branches of mathematics are based in part on propositions that are not provable within the system itself, although they may be proved by logical systems external to themselves. Gödel's "incompleteness theorem" demonstrates that an infinitude of propositions

that are underivable from the axioms of a system nevertheless have the value of truth within the system.

10. A logical principle of parsimony, demanding economy in
explanation. Occam's Razor states, "What can be done with
fewer assumptions is done in vain with more."

INVENTORS

1. Benjamin Franklin (1706–90). The great American statesman,
printer, and writer was also a great scientist. Among his
inventions were bifocals, the lightning rod, the Franklin
stove, and a glass harmonica.
2. James Watt (1736–1819). A new type of engine with a separate condensing chamber, an air pump to bring steam into
the chamber, and with parts of the engine insulated was
patented by Watt in 1769. Watt coined the term *horsepower*,
and the unit of electrical power was named for him.
3. Galileo Galilei (1564–1642). In 1609 he constructed the first
complete astronomical telescope. With its use he greatly
enlarged humanity's vision and conception of the universe.
4. Thomas Edison (1847–1931). Edison's phonograph, patented
in 1878, was notable as the first successful instrument of its
kind.
5. Thomas Edison. He created the first commercially practical
incandescent lamp in 1879. Edison was a genius in the practical application of scientific principles.
6. The passenger elevator. Elisha Otis (1811–61) invented the
automatic safety device that prevented the fall of hoisting
machinery in 1852. The invention permitted the building of
skyscrapers.
7. The reaper. In 1831 Cyrus McCormick (1809–94) first demon-
strated the reaping innovations that are the essentials of
every satisfactory harvesting machine. In 1847 he built his
Chicago factory. In 1851 he introduced his reaper into England, and subsequently into other European countries.
8. Radio. Guglielmo Marconi (1874–1937) transmitted long-
wave signals over a distance of more than a mile in 1895. In
1901 he transmitted the first transatlantic wireless signals.
9. The printing press. Johann Gutenberg (c. 1397–1468) is

believed to have been the first European to print with movable types cast in molds. His printing in quantity work of excellent quality contributed significantly to the technology of human communication.

10. The cotton gin. Eli Whitney (1765–1825) completed a model gin that separated the fiber of short-staple cotton from its seed in 1793. His patent was not renewed after 1812, and the invention, which brought great wealth to others, brought little to Whitney himself.

NOVELISTS

1. Jane Austen, the English novelist (1775–1817). Her name did not appear on any of her title pages, and she received little public recognition in her lifetime.
2. Feodor Dostoyevsky, the Russian novelist (1821–81). *Crime and Punishment* (1866) is a brilliant portrait of sin, remorse, and redemption through sacrifice.
3. Leo Tolstoy, the Russian novelist (1828–1910). *War and Peace* (1865–69) is a vast prose epic of the Napoleonic invasion of 1812, with a stream of brilliantly conceived characters and incidents.
4. Mark Twain, the American author (1835–1910). In the hero of *Huckleberry Finn* (1884), a resourceful, unconventional boy with an innate sense of human values, Twain created one of the most memorable characters in fiction.
5. Harriet Beecher Stowe, the American novelist (1811–96). In *Uncle Tom's Cabin* (1852), Stowe helped to stir the conscience of Americans about slavery and thereby influenced the course of American history.
6. *Invisible Man* (1952). Ellison's novel details the harrowing progress of a nameless young black man trying to find a place for himself in a hostile society.
7. *Madame Bovary* (1856). Flaubert was prosecuted on moral grounds after its publication, but he won the case.
8. *The Great Gatsby* (1925). Cynical yet poignant, the novel is a devastating portrait of the so-called American Dream, which measures success and love in terms of money.
9. *The Mystery of Edwin Drood*. Dickens died in 1870 after a

series of exhausting reading tours in America and England.
10. *The Awakening* (1899). After the criticism of her novel, Chopin was largely ignored for sixty years. Now her work is praised for its literary merit as well as for its remarkable independence of mind and feeling.

COMPOSERS

1. Wolfgang Amadeus Mozart, the Austrian composer (1756–91). *Eine Kleine Nachtmusik* ("A Little Night Music," 1787) is a serenade for strings. It was written for a social occasion.
2. Johann Sebastian Bach (1685–1750), the German composer. The *Brandenburg Concertos* are six concerti grossi.
3. Antonio Vivaldi (1675?–1741), the Italian composer. *The Four Seasons* are concerti grossi. Vivaldi also wrote 447 concertos for violin and other instruments.
4. Peter Ilyich Tchaikovsky (1848–93), the Russian composer. He also arranged the ballet music for *The Nutcracker* as a suite for orchestra.
5. George Frideric Handel (1685–1759), the English composer. He composed the *Water Music* for King George I.
6. *The Rite of Spring* (*Le sacre du printemps*). Igor Stravinsky (1882–1971) used irregular, primitive rhythms and harsh dissonances in the score of the ballet music. A year after its riotous debut in Paris, the work was performed by a symphony orchestra and recognized as a masterpiece of modern music.
7. The Ring Cycle, or *Der Ring des Nibelungen* (1853–74). Richard Wagner (1813–83) wrote as well as composed his operas. He built a theater in Bayreuth in which to stage his works, especially the Ring Cycle.
8. The *Eroica* (1803–1804). Ludwig van Beethoven (1770–1827) originally dedicated this massive landmark work to Napoleon, who at first symbolized to him the spirit of the French Revolution; but when Napoleon proclaimed himself emperor, the disillusioned composer renamed the work the "Heroic Symphony to celebrate the memory of a great man."
9. *Carmen* (1875). The opera by Georges Bizet (1838–75) is a

story of love, hate, jealousy, and murder, with music that is lush, melodic, and brilliantly orchestrated.

10. The *Unfinished* (1822). The work was not the composer's last symphony. Franz Schubert (1797–1828) composed a ninth in 1828.

PAINTERS

1. Leonardo da Vinci (1452–1519). Leonardo painted her in the early 1500s. She was the wife of a Florentine merchant.

2. Claude Monet (1840–1926) painted the great lyrical series of water lilies in his own garden at Giverny during the last twenty-five years of his life.

3. Andy Warhol (1930–1987) chose many of his commonplace subjects from the worlds of advertising and product consumerism. Monotony and repetition became the hallmark of his multi-image, mass-produced silk-screen paintings.

4. Pablo Picasso (1881–1973). *Les Demoiselles d'Avignon* (1907) was a radical departure from the artistic ideas of the preceding ages and is now considered the most significant work in the development toward cubism and modern abstraction.

5. Michelangelo Buonarotti (1475–1564). Michelangelo painted the ceiling of the Sistine Chapel in Rome for Pope Julius II between 1508 and 1512. In its profundity of spiritual content and in its sublimity of style, the work stands as one of the world's greatest masterpieces.

6. *Nude Descending a Staircase*. Marcel Duchamp (1887–1968) also invented ready-mades—commonplace objects that he exhibited as works of art (e.g., the urinal entitled *Fountain*).

7. *American Gothic*. Grant Wood (1891–1942) is noted for his "American scene" works in which severe people and stylized landscapes offer rigid decorative images of the rural Midwest in the 1930s.

8. *Christina's World*. Andrew Wyeth (b. 1917) painted places and people in Maine in a meticulous naturalistic style. They are so intensely and immediately rendered as to appear surreal.

9. *The Persistence of Memory*. Salvador Dalí (1904–89) was a leader of surrealism. His precise style enhanced the nightmare effect of his paintings.

10. *Arrangement in Gray and Black.* As part of a vigorous campaign to propagate his credo of art for art's sake, J. A. M. Whistler (1834–1903) gave many of his works abstract titles to de-emphasize their subjective content and to play up the significance of their harmonious arrangement of light, form, and color.

MOVIE PEOPLE

1. Orson Welles (1915–85). Welles wrote, produced, directed, and starred in the movie. It is noted for its technical brilliance, structural complexity, and literate treatment of a controversial biographical subject.
2. Cary Grant (1904–86) and Katharine Hepburn (b. 1907). Grant expressed to perfection the essence of debonair British charm and elegance in several comic-romantic leading roles. Hepburn remained a strikingly individual and commanding presence on the screen from 1932.
3. Akira Kurosawa (b. 1910). The Japanese director followed *Rashomon*, about truth and illusion, with *Ikiru* (1952), a moving study of an elderly bureaucrat facing death by cancer.
4. Ingmar Bergman (b. 1918). The Swedish film and stage writer, director, and producer had complete control over most of his films, working within small budgets, with a small group of players and technicians whom he used repeatedly in films and stage works.
5. Laurence Olivier (1907–89). Olivier is often referred to as the greatest actor of the twentieth century. He also starred in *Henry V* (1944), *Hamlet* (1948), *Richard III* (1956), *The Entertainer* (1960), *Othello* (1965), and other movies.
6. *The Godfather.* Parts 1 and 2 received the 1972 and 1974 Oscars, respectively, for Best Picture. Part 3 (1990) completed this study of an Italian-American crime family.
7. *Casablanca.* Bogart became famous for his portrayals of tough, cynical heroes, while Bergman specialized in portraits of strong, dignified, and sophisticated women.
8. *Anna Karenina.* After her successful portrayals of sexual pas-

sion and tragic heroism in two decades of movies, Garbo (1905–89) retired from the screen in 1941 and lived in legendary seclusion for the rest of her life.

9. *Who's Afraid of Virginia Woolf?* Burton (1925–84) and Taylor (b. 1932) married each other twice.

10. Switzerland. Chaplin (1889–1977) had been criticized by the American press and government for his politics and personal behavior.

SPORTS FIGURES

1. O. J. Simpson. The American football player (b. 1947) had a career record of 11,236 yards gained rushing, which ranks second only to that of Jimmy Brown.

2. Lou Gehrig. The disease killed the American baseball player (1903–41) at age thirty-seven. He had a lifetime batting average of .340, hit 493 home runs, and batted .361 in seven World Series.

3. Martina Navratilova. The Czech-American tennis player (b. 1956) is the all-time leader in international tournament victories (158).

4. Muhammad Ali. The American boxer, born Cassius Marcellus Clay in 1942, changed his name when he became a Black Muslim. He won an Olympic gold medal in 1960, and defeated Sonny Liston in 1964 for the world heavyweight crown. When he refused induction into the army on religious grounds, he was stripped of the title in 1967. In 1971 the Supreme Court upheld his draft appeal. He won the heavyweight title for the third time in 1978 (from Spinks).

5. Wilt Chamberlain. The American basketball player (b. 1936) is famed for his long-standing rivalry with Boston's Bill Russell and for his record 100 points scored against the New York Knicks.

6. The Boston Red Sox. The American baseball player (b. 1918) was one of the finest natural hitters the game has ever known. He batted .406 in 1941.

7. The heptathlon and the long jump. The American athlete (b. 1962) set the world heptathlon record.

8. Johnson stunned the nation with his announcement that he had tested positive for the AIDS virus.
9. The Los Angeles Kings. The Canadian ice hockey player (b. 1961) had been playing for the Edmonton Oilers. In 1981–82 he set single-season NHL marks for goals scored (92), assists (120), and points (212), becoming the first player to achieve more than 200 points.
10. Brazil. Pelé (b. 1940) led Brazil to world championships in 1958, 1962, and 1970. His playing style was marked by superb ball control and great technical ability.

GREAT THINKERS

1. Plato (427?–347 B.C.). He asserted that philosophers were the only ones capable of ruling the just state, since through their study of dialectic they understood the harmony of all parts of the universe in relation to the Idea of the Good.
2. Karl Heinrich Marx (1818–83). The *Communist Manifesto* was published in 1848. Marx's later monumental *Das Kapital* (3 vols.: 1867, 1885, and 1894) became the foundation of international socialism.
3. Charles Darwin (1809–82) first presented his idea of evolution by natural selection to the general public in his famous book in 1859. Independently, A. R. Wallace had worked out a theory similar to Darwin's.
4. Adam Smith (1723–90). *The Wealth of Nations* was published in 1776. As an analyst of institutions and an early advocate of the free-market system, Smith laid the foundation for the classic system of economics. His influence on later economists has never been surpassed.
5. Sigmund Freud (1856–1939). *The Interpretation of Dreams* was published in 1900 and translated into English in 1913. His psychoanalytic theories of the unconscious mind have had an extraordinary impact, influencing such diverse fields as anthropology, education, art, and literature.
6. *Confessions* (1782). The influential ideas of philosopher and political theorist Jean Jacques Rousseau (1712–78) begin with the assumption that humanity is by nature good, and with the further observation that in society humanity is not good.

7. *Il Principe* (*The Prince*). Published in 1532 (but written in 1513), Machiavelli's work has been variously viewed as cynical but sincere advice, as a plea for political office, as a detached analysis of Italian politics, as evidence of early Italian nationalism, and as political satire on Medici rule.

8. Aristotle (384–322 B.C.) He considered philosophy to be the discerning of the self-evident, changeless first principles that form the basis of all knowledge. Logic was for him the necessary tool of any inquiry, and the syllogism was the sequence that a logical thought follows.

9. Ludwig Wittgenstein (1889–1951). His first major work was the *Tractatus Logico-philosophicus* (1921). His later work is represented by *Philosophical Investigations* (1953).

10. The *Encyclopédie*. The work epitomized the spirit of the Enlightenment. Diderot (1713–84) took on its editorship in 1745, with the first volume published in 1751. He lived to see the project completed in 1772. Of the twenty-eight volumes, eleven were devoted to plates illustrating the industrial arts. Diderot compiled this information and made the drawings. In page proof, Diderot found that the printer had mutilated many articles by deleting liberal opinions.

SPIRITUAL LEADERS

1. Moses. The Torah (or the Pentateuch, or first five books of the Bible) is believed by Orthodox Jews to have been handed to Moses on Mount Sinai in the thirteenth century B.C. Many critics deny the Mosaic authorship of the books.

2. Jesus Christ, or Jesus of Nazareth (c. 6 B.C.–A.D. 30). Matthew was a tax collector, Luke a doctor. Other early accounts of Jesus' life are by Mark and John.

3. Muhammad (570?–632). The canonical text was established A.H. 30 (A.D. 651–52),under the caliph Uthman, by Arabic editors, who used for their basis a collection made by Zaid ibn Thabit, the Prophet's secretary.

4. Confucius, or K'ung Fu-tzu (c. 551–479 B.C.).The *Analects* are a collection of sayings and short dialogues apparently collected by Confucius's disciples. The *Wu Ching* (Five Classics) are also traditionally attributed to him.

5. Lao-Tse, or Lao-Tsu (b. ca. 604 B.C.). It is uncertain that he is historical. Legend describes him as a librarian at the Chou court. But the text must have actually been composed several centuries after his supposed lifetime.
6. The Sutra. Buddha lived c. 563–483 B.C. The Buddhist canon was formulated and transmitted by oral tradition; it was gradually written down in several versions over the course of the second and first centuries B.C. Its main divisions, called *pitakas* (baskets), are the Vinaya or monastic rules, the Sutra (Pali *Sutta*) or discourses of the Buddha, and the Abhidharma (Pali *abhidhamma*) or scholastic metaphysics.
7. The Indian National Congress. Throughout his adult life, Mohandas Karamchand "Mahatma" Gandhi (1869–1948) asserted the unity of mankind under one God, preaching Christian and Muslim ethics along with Hindu.
8. Gabon (formerly French Equatorial Africa). Albert Schweitzer (1875–1965) was awarded the 1952 Nobel Peace Prize.
9. Montgomery, Alabama. Martin Luther King, Jr. (1929–68) also organized the 1963 March on Washington. He was awarded the 1964 Nobel Peace Prize.
10. Calcutta. In 1948 Mother Teresa (born Agnes Gonxha Bojaxhiu in 1910) founded the Missionaries of Charity, which now operates schools, hospitals, orphanages, and food centers in over twenty-five countries. She was awarded the 1979 Nobel Peace Prize.

MILITARY LEADERS

1. George Washington (1732–99). Washington made the American Revolution successful not only by his personal military triumphs but also by his skill in directing other operations. At the war's end he was the most important man in the country. In 1789 he was unanimously chosen the first president of the United States.
2. Ulysses S. Grant (1822–85). The Vicksburg Campaign (1862–63) was one of his greatest successes. Grant became the eighteenth president of the United States (1869–77).
3. Robert E. Lee (1807–70). Many historians regard Lee as the

greatest general of the Civil War. After the war he became president of Washington College (now Washington and Lee University) in Lexington, Virginia.

4. Dwight David Eisenhower (1890–1969). Eisenhower later served as president of Columbia University (1948). He became the thirty-fourth president of the United States (1953–61). During his second term Eisenhower took the initiative in the growing civil rights movement.

5. Norman Schwarzkopf (b. 1934). He retired from the U.S. Army in 1992 as a four-star general and wrote his autobiography.

6. Erwin Rommel (1891–1944), fighting for Germany, earned his name and rank of field marshall after his successes with the Afrika Korps in Libya in 1941. Because of his part in the July 1944 attempt on Hitler's life, he was forced to take poison.

7. Carthage. Hannibal (247–183 B.C.)crossed the Pyrenees, then the Alps with elephants and a full baggage train. He won a brilliant victory at Cannae in 216, but never managed to attack Rome.

8. England. Saladin (1137 or 1138–1193), the Muslim warrior and sultan of Egypt (1174), captured Jerusalem in 1187. The confrontation between Saladin and Richard I (the "Lion Heart") of England was to be celebrated in later chivalric romance. Saladin was a learned man and a great patron of the arts.

9. Italy. Giuseppe Garibaldi (1807–82) led one thousand "Red Shirts" in a spectacular conquest of Sicily and Naples in 1860. He was elected to the Italian parliament in 1874.

10. Korea (or South Korea). Douglas MacArthur (1880–1964) fought in both world wars and directed the postwar occupation of Japan. During the Korean War he became involved in a policy dispute with President Truman, who removed him from command in 1951.

POLITICAL LEADERS

1. Sir Winston Churchill (1874–1965). The British supported the vigorous program of his coalition cabinet until after the surrender of Germany. Then in July 1945, British desire for rapid

social reform led to a Labour electoral victory, and Churchill became leader of the opposition.

2. Boris Yeltsin (b. 1931). He was elected Russian president in June 1991. By August he had presided over the dissolution of the Communist party and the Soviet Union.

3. Fidel Castro (b. 1926). After assuming the premiership of Cuba, he established a totalitarian government that benefited the working class at the expense of the middle class, many of whom fled. He nationalized industry, confiscated property, and collectivized agriculture.

4. Lech Walesa (b. 1943). He was elected president of Poland in 1990.

5. Oliver Cromwell (1599–1658). In the period following the king's execution in 1649, Cromwell became virtual dictator of the republican Commonwealth of England, Scotland, and Ireland. From 1653 to 1658 his official title was lord protector (he refused the crown in 1657).

6. South Africa. In prison Mandela (b. 1918) became the leading symbol of South African repression. He was released in 1990, and was elected president of the African National Congress in 1991.

7. India. Jawaharlal Nehru (1889–1964) participated in the negotiations that created an independent India in 1947 and served as its prime minister until his death. His daughter Indira Gandhi also later became prime minister of the country.

8. Vietnam (later, North Vietnam). Ho Chi Minh (1890–1969) fought against the Japanese during World War II, then campaigned against the restored French colonial government until 1954, when the Geneva Conference divided the country into communist North Vietnam and noncommunist South Vietnam. Ho served as the first president of North Vietnam (from 1954 to 1969), during which time America's gradually increasing support of South Vietnam led to the Vietnam War.

9. France. Cardinal Richelieu (1585–1642) destroyed the political power of the Huguenots by 1628 and helped make France Europe's leading power. He founded the French Academy.

10. Prussia (premier) and Germany (chancellor). Otto von Bismarck (1815–98), known as the "Iron Chancellor," was virtual dictator of the German empire for nearly twenty years.

CONQUERORS, EMPERORS, DICTATORS

1. Napoleon Bonaparte, or Napoleon I (1769–1821), emperor of the French (1804–14). While he is one of history's great conquerors, he also promoted the growth of liberalism through valuable and lasting administrative and legal reforms, notably the Code Napoléon, which is still the basis of French law.
2. Adolf Hitler (1889–1945), Austrian-born German dictator (1933–45). His legacy is the memory of the most dreadful tyranny of modern times: the German Third Reich, which systematically executed over six million European Jews and others in the Holocaust.
3. Joseph Stalin (1879–1953). He adopted this name ("man of steel") about 1913. He made his Soviet dictatorship absolute by liquidating all opposition within the Communist party. It was not until 1956 that he was denounced publicly in Russia, by Nikita Krushchev, for tyranny, terror, falsification of history, and self-glorification.
4. Charlemagne, or Charles the Great (742?–814). His achievements and prestige were of such magnitude that later generations enlarged them to fantastic proportions. It was Charlemagne's example that Napoleon had in mind when he had himself crowned emperor by the pope in 1804.
5. Genghis Khan (1167?–1227), the Mongol conqueror. His wars were marked by ruthless carnage, but he was a brilliant ruler and military leader.
6. The Macedonians. Alexander (356–323 B.C.), king of Macedonia and conqueror of the Persian empire, was one of the greatest leaders of all time. His empire stretched east to north India, and his conquests prepared the way for the Hellenistic age.
7. The Persians. Cyrus II (the Great; d. 529 B.C.)figures prominently in the Bible and was admired as a liberator rather than a conqueror because he respected the customs and religions of each part of his empire.
8. The Huns. The fear that Attila, the "Scourge of God" (d. 453), inspired is clear from many accounts of his savagery, but he was a just, if harsh, ruler to his own people, and he encouraged the presence of learned Romans at his court.
9. The Mongols. Tamerlane, or Timur the Lame (c. 1336–1405) was cruel: after capturing certain cities he slaughtered thou-

sands of their defenders (perhaps 80,000 at Delhi) and built pyramids of their skulls.'But he also encouraged art, literature, and science, and the construction of vast public works. He claimed to be descended from Genghis Khan.

10. The Aztecs. Montezuma II's rule (c. 1502–20) was marked by incessant warfare, and his despotism caused grave unrest among subject peoples. Cortés, the Spanish explorer and conqueror of Mexico, seized him as a hostage and attempted to govern through him. Montezuma was killed in an Aztec uprising.

LEGENDARY FIGURES

1. Oedipus, king of Thebes. In Greek legend he unwittingly fulfilled the oracle's prophecy, killed his father, and married his mother Jocasta. When he learned the truth he blinded himself. The story is best told in tragedies by the Athenian dramatist Sophocles.

2. Guinevere. In Arthurian legend her illicit and tragic love for Sir Lancelot ends with her retirement to a convent. The best-known recent versions of the story are T. H. White's *The Once and Future King* (1958) and Alan Jay Lerner and Frederick Loewe's musical, *Camelot* (1960).

3. Samson. In the Bible story (probably drawn from popular oral folktales), Samson's hair, worn long because of an agreement with God, gives him strength. His enemies the Philistines persuade Delilah, his wife, to cut his hair, thus breaking his vow and causing him to become weak. Sampson is blinded and chained, but gradually his strength returns as his hair grows back. Brought to a crowded Philistine temple to be publicly humiliated in defeat, Sampson calls on God's help and brings the temple down on himself and his enemies.

4. Hiawatha. He is the hero of the well-known poem by Henry Wadsworth Longfellow, *The Song of Hiawatha* (1855).

5. Prester John. The legend first appeared in the twelfth century and persisted for several centuries. Letters supposedly written by and about him were widely circulated in Western Europe.

6. **He charmed away Hamelin's children.** In the thirteenth-century legend, the Pied Piper rid Hamelin of its rats by charming them away with his flute-playing. When he was refused payment, he charmed away the town's children. The story has been immortalized by Goethe, Robert Browning, and the Brothers Grimm.

7. **She rode naked on a white horse.** In the eleventh-century English legend, Godiva's husband agreed to remit the heavy taxation on the people of Coventry (which he and she founded in 1043) if she would ride naked through the town on a white horse. The story of Peeping Tom, the only person who supposedly looked at her (through the closed shutters) when she did this, did not enter the legend until the seventeenth century.

8. **He sold his soul to the devil.** In the sixteenth-century German legend, Faust sold his soul to the devil Mephistopheles in exchange for youth, knowledge, and magical power. The story has inspired great works of literature by Marlowe, Goethe, and Thomas Mann and great works of music by Berlioz, Gounod, Liszt, and Schumann.

9. **He shot an apple off his son's head.** In Swiss legend, this fourteenth-century hero was ordered to shoot an apple off his son's head by Gessler, the Austrian bailiff of Tell's forest canton. Tell succeeds and later kills Gessler.

10. **He died competing against a steam drill.** In this nineteenth-century African-American legend, John Henry tries to outwork the steam drill with only his hammer and steel bit. He beats the drill but dies of the strain. His legend originated about 1870 among The miners drilling the Big Bend Tunnel of the Chesapeake and Ohio Railway in West Virginia and may have some historical basis.

FICTIONAL CHARACTERS

1. **Hamlet.** Complex, cerebral, and brooding, this character would not be half so interesting if he could, like Laertes, act in the heat of passion.

2. **Hercule Poirot.** The other great detective created by Agatha Christie is Jane Marple, the elderly spinster.

3. Count Dracula. *Dracula* (1897) is the most famous novel by Bram Stoker (1847–1912), who for twenty-seven years was the manager of the actor Sir Henry Irving.
4. Holden Caulfield. Salinger's *The Catcher in the Rye* (1951) was extremely popular among high school and college students of the 1950s and 1960s.
5. Sam Spade, notably in *The Maltese Falcon* (1930). The other famous character in the "hard-boiled," realistic, fast-paced stories of Hammett (1894–1961) was Nick Charles, notably in *The Thin Man* (1932).
6. William Shakespeare (1564–1616). Falstaff in *Henry IV* would not be so beloved if, in addition to being genial, open-hearted, and witty, he were not also boisterous, cowardly, and, ultimately, poignant.
7. Charles M. Schultz (b. 1922). Charlie Brown and Snoopy are two principal characters in Schultz's comic strip "Peanuts."
8. A. Milne (1882–1956). *Winnie-the-Pooh* (1926) and *The House at Pooh Corner* (1928) established the characters Christopher Robin and his toy animal friends Pooh Bear, Piglet, and Eeyore.
9. Charles Dickens (1812–70), in the story *A Christmas Carol* (1843). For generations of readers, the names of his characters—including David Copperfield, Oliver Twist, Ebenezer Scrooge, Mr. Pickwick, Uriah Heep, Miss Haversham—have been household words.
10. Beatrix Potter (1866–1943). This British author published her first book about Peter Rabbit in 1902 at her own expense. Her twenty-three books, all illustrated by herself, are now considered children's classics.

GODS

1. Zeus. He was the symbol of power, rule, and law. He rewarded the good and punished the evil. His most famous weapon was the thunderbolt. The Romans equated him with their own supreme god, Jupiter (or Jove).
2. Gaea. She was the earth, daughter of Chaos, mother and wife of Uranus, the sky, and Pontus, the sea.

3. Mars (Ares to the Greeks). He was the father of Romulus, the founder of the Roman nation, and, next to Jupiter, he enjoyed the highest position in Roman religion. His priests danced in full armor in the Campus Martius, the site of his altar. The month of March is named for him.

4. Vishnu, the preserver god. Usually considered the primal god in the Hindu sacred triad (with Brahma, the god of creation, and Siva, the god of destruction and regeneration), he is generally depicted as dark blue in color, crowned, and bearing in his four hands his emblems—the conch, discus, mace, and lotus. His many avatars include Krishna and Rama.

5. Woden (or Odin, in Norse mythology). He was attended at his court at Valhalla by the Valkyries and is perhaps most famously depicted in the four operas that make up Wagner's Ring cycle. Wednesday is named for him.

6. Ancient Greek. It was to Aphrodite, goddess of love and beauty, that Paris awarded the apple of discord, which caused the dispute leading ultimately to the Trojan War.

7. Aztec. Huitzilopochtli (also god of the sun) was usually represented in sculptured images as hideous. He was the object of human sacrifice, particularly of war prisoners. His temple at Tenochtitlán (present-day Mexico City) was a great architectural achievement of pre-Columbian America.

8. Babylonian and Assyrian. Ishtar was their most widely worshiped goddess. As a mother goddess and goddess of love, she was the source of all the generative powers in nature and mankind. However, she was also a goddess of war, and as such was capable of unremitting cruelty.

9. Ancient Egyptian. Isis was frequently represented with a cow's head or cow's horns. Her brother and husband was Osiris.

10. Ancient Persian. Mithra (or Mithras in Latin and Greek) was god of light and wisdom. His cult expanded to become a worldwide religion, Mithraism, which in the second century A.D. was more general in the late Roman empire than Christianity, to which it bore many similarities.

ANIMALS

1. The bat. There are between one thousand and two thousand species of bat, ranging in size from a wingspread of more than five feet to a wingspread of less than two inches.
2. The oyster. Pearls are secretions formed inside an oyster's shell around an irritant.
3. The skunk. The liquid it propels from under its tail produces a fine mist with a highly offensive odor.
4. The cuckoo. Old World female cuckoos lay eggs in other birds' nests, and the young, which are larger than their nest mates, displace them from the nest and become the sole recipients of their foster parents' care. To cuckold someone is to mate with his wife (i.e., to displace him).
5. The Pekingese. The breed is believed to have existed in its present form as early as the eighth century, when it was kept as a palace dog by the Chinese emperors. When its breeding was guarded by the court, the punishment for stealing a Pekingese was death.
6. The elephant. Ivory from elephant tusks has been prized for its appearance and texture since ancient times and is an excellent material for carving. The threatened extinction of elephants, to a large extent the result of wholesale slaughter for tusks, and the resulting increased costs of ivory, have encouraged the making of imitations.
7. Mules are sterile. They are themselves the hybrid offspring of male donkeys and female horses.
8. Reptiles. They were egg-laying animals, ranging in length from two and half feet to about ninety feet.
9. The sponge. Its skeleton is cleaned of living tissue, dried, and processed, making it capable of holding water.
10. The echidna (Australia, Tasmania, New Guinea) and the

platypus (Australia, Tasmania). They are the only two members of the most primitive order of mammals, the monotremes.

PLANTS

1. An apple. Another fateful apple was the golden one given by Paris to Aphrodite, settling a dispute between Hera (who offered him greatness and wealth), Athena (who offered him success in war), and Aphrodite (who offered him Helen, the most beautiful woman in the world). Paris's abduction of Helen started the Trojan War.
2. An acorn. Acorns, one of the most important foods among the forest Native Americans, were pulverized, leached to extract the bitter taste, and then cooked in various ways.
3. Ebony. Its wood is hard and dark. Macassar ebony from India and the East Indies is extensively used for pianos and cabinetmaking. Persimmon wood, also called ebony and belonging to the same genus as true ebony, is used for golf club heads.
4. Hemp (or cannabis). Its fiber is also used in making paper, cloth, and other products. The chemical derived from flower clusters and top leaves of the female plant is the source of the powerful (but physically nonaddictive) narcotics marijuana and hashish.
5. The lotus. The flower (a water lily) is traditional in Egyptian art and architecture (for instance, in the lotus capital of a column). The Indian lotus is sacred in Hinduism and Buddhism.
6. The olive. The olive branch has been a symbol of peace since ancient times because the oil could be used both to heal human ills and to calm troubled waters.
7. The laurel. Native to the Mediterranean, it symbolized victory and merit to the ancients. Hence the laurel wreath or crown.
8. Papyrus. Now almost extinct in Egypt, it was so universally used there that its hieroglyphic was the symbol for Lower Egypt. It was used as fuel, food, and to make cloth, but most notably to make a writing material.

9. Truffles. These gastronomical delicacies (genus *Tuber*) grow close to the roots of trees in woodlands, particularly near Perigord, France.
10. These plants are all carniverous. Probably the best-known carniverous plant is the Venus's-flytrap, whose leaves are hinged at the midrib, each half bearing sensitive bristles. When a bristle is touched by an insect, the halves snap shut and the marginal t eeth interlock to imprison the insect until it is digested.

ELEMENTS, MINERALS, AND METALS

1. Oxygen. It constitutes about half of the total material of the earth's surface. Most of this oxygen is combined in the form of silicates, oxides, and water. It makes up about 90 percent of water, two-thirds of the human body, and one-fifth by volume of air.
2. Hydrogen. It is only about one part per million in the atmosphere, but it is believed to make up about three quarters of the mass of the universe, or over 90 percent of the molecules. It is the least dense gas known.
3. Carbon. Carbon exists in the stars. It is also a constituent of all organic matter. Plastics, food, textiles, and many other common substances contain carbon.
4. Diamond. It is one of the two crystalline forms of carbon, the other one being graphite, which is greasy and soft.
5. Copper. The greenish film is called patina. The coating protects the metal from further attack.
6. Lead. Another of its many uses is in dampening vibrations. It was used in the foundations of the Pan Am Building built over Grand Central Station in New York City.
7. Twenty-four. A carat is one twenty-fourth by weight of the total mass of the metal. Eighteen-carat gold is a 75 percent alloy.
8. Pumice. Because of its air chambers, pumice has a very low density and has been observed blowing off volcanic islands in strong winds. It usually floats and can be carried great distances by ocean currents.

9. The shells of minute animals called foraminifera. Chalk has been laid down in all periods of geologic time, but most of the best-known deposits (e.g., the cliffs of the English Channel) date from the Cretaceous period, about 140 to 165 million years ago.

10. Plants. The vegetable origin of coal is supported by the presence in coal of carbonized fibers, stems, leaves, and seeds of plants, which can be seen with the naked eye in the softer varieties.

WEIRD BEASTS

1. In Greek mythology the Sphinx was a winged female monster with a woman's head and a lion's body who killed anyone unable to answer its riddle. In ancient Egypt a sphinx was a mythical beast usually represented in a recumbent position with the head of a man and the body of a lion (though some were constructed with rams' heads and others with hawks' heads).

2. According to ancient legend, the phoenix lived in Arabia. When it died after five hundred years, it burned itself on a pyre of flames, and from the ashes a new phoenix arose.

3. The coelacanth is the nearest living fish relative of the amphibians. Thought to be extinct until 1938 when a live one was caught in deep water off South Africa, it is a brown to steel-blue fish five feet long, with circular, overlapping scales, a laterally flattened three-lobed tail, a spiny dorsal fin, and a vestigial lung.

4. The unicorn, a fabulous equine creature with a horn jutting from its forehead, is usually depicted as pure white and often represents virginity. Hunting the unicorn was a common subject in tapestries of the late Middle Ages and Renaissance.

5. The pterodactyl was a flying reptile. Fossils of about twenty-nine species of these extinct creatures have been found, ranging in size from that of a sparrow to that of a dragonlike creature with a wingspread of more than twenty feet.

6. A golem. The most famous legend centers around Rabbi Low of sixteenth-century Prague, who was forced to destroy the golem he had formed and endowed with life after it ran amok.

7. The Minotaur, a monster with the head of a bull and the body of a man. The craftsman Daedalus constructed the labyrinth to confine the beast.
8. A Harpy. The Harpies snatched food from tables or else befouled tables, leaving filth and stench and causing famine.
9. A griffin. It is often found in Persian sculpture and decorative arts.
10. A werewolf. In the Middle Ages the church condemned werewolves as sorcerers and often ruthlessly punished supposed offenders.

OUTER SPACE

1. Magnetic storms on the surface of the sun. They usually appear between 5 and 35 degrees north and south of the sun's equator, and particularly in periods of activity about eleven years apart.
2. A star that is abnormally faint for its white-hot temperature. A typical white dwarf has the mass of the sun and the radius of the earth.
3. A star that is unusually cool for its luminosity and size. A red giant's condition results from its having converted its hydrogen atoms to helium: its central core contracts, and its outer layers expand and cool. Very large red giants have diameters one hundred to one thousand times that of the sun.
4. The theoretically predicted final stage in a star's gravitational collapse. When the star shrinks below a certain size determined by its mass, even light cannot escape the enormous pull of its gravitation. For a collapsed star with a mass equal to that of the sun, the diameter of its invisible sphere would be 1.8 miles.
5. A quasi-stellar radio source, currently believed to be the most distant and most luminous type of object in the universe. Quasars may be many billion light-years away, and as luminous intrinsically as a thousand galaxies combined.
6. A nebula. Some nebulas emit their own light, some reflect light, some do neither and are seen as empty patches in a field of stars or as clouds obscuring part of a bright nebula in the background.

7. Nothing. A comet's tail is pushed by the solar wind away from the sun, whichever direction the comet is flying. It follows the comet's head as the comet approaches the sun and precedes it as the comet moves away from the sun.

8. Asteroids (sometimes called planetoids or minor planets) Ceres is the largest, with a diameter of about 470 miles. More than two thousand have been tracked and cataloged; thousands more exist.

9. Meteors. When they become visible they are "shooting stars" or "falling stars" and are often observable at the rate of five to ten per hour. More meteors are visible after midnight (local time) because the earth's rotation has then positioned the observer's part of the earth in the direction of the earth's motion about the sun. Meteors that reach the earth's surface intact are called meteorites.

10. A supernova. Over 120 extended galactic radio sources have been identified as supernova remnants. Of these only five have been positively associated with explosions that were optically observed in recorded history. They occurred in 1006, 1054, 1572, 1604, and 1987.

UNIQUE THINGS

1. The great fracture in the earth's crust in California extending more than six hundred miles from northwest California to the gulf of California. Movement along the fault causes earthquakes, some of them severe.

2. The boundary between Pennsylvania and Maryland surveyed by English astronomers Charles Mason and Jeremiah Dixon between 1763 and 1767. Before the Civil War the term popularly designated the boundary dividing the slave states from the free states, and it is still used to distinguish the North from the South.

3. Ancient sculptures taken from Athens, Greece, in 1806 by Lord Elgin. The Parthenon frieze by Phidias, a caryatid, and a column from the Erechtheum were sold to the British government in 1816 and are on view in the British Museum.

4. A slab inscribed with identical texts in Greek and ancient Egyptian hieroglyphs that provided the key to deciphering

Egyptian hieroglyphics. Found by Napoleon's troops at Rosetta, Egypt, in 1799, it was brought to England by the British in 1801 and is now in the British Museum.

5. The sword given to King Arthur in Arthurian legend by the Lady of the Lake. At Arthur's death Sir Bedivere threw Excalibur into the lake; a hand rose from the water, caught the sword, and disappeared.
6. The Great Rift Valley. Erosion has concealed some sections of the long rift system, but in other places, notably Kenya, there are sheer cliffs several thousand feet high.
7. The Wailing Wall. It is a holy place for Jews.
8. The Dead Sea Scrolls. Among the scrolls are two copies, one complete, the other incomplete, of the Book of Isaiah which are one thousand years older than any biblical manuscript known before.
9. The Holy Grail. Connected with many tales of crusading knights (including Arthurian legend), the Grail could miraculously provide food and healing but would be revealed only to a pure knight. These stories have inspired many works of art, literature, and music, including Wagner's operas *Lohengrin* (1848) and *Parsifal* (1882).
10. The Peacock Throne. It is now in a museum in Teheran, where it was brought by Nadir Shah in 1739.

SCIENTIFIC INSTRUMENTS

1. Measuring temperature. Clinical thermometers use mercury as the heat-measuring medium in small tubes of thick glass.
2. Detecting and recording earthquakes. Generally a heavy mass, either a pendulum or a large permanent magnet, is an essential part of the detecting instrument.
3. Measuring atmospheric pressure. The barometer was invented in 1643 by the Italian scientist Evangelista Torricelli (1608–47).
4. Detecting the position and nature of a remote object by means of radio waves reflected from its surface. It was developed in the 1930s independently in several countries.
5. Recording and interpreting the electrical activity that precedes and is a measure of the action of heart muscles. It is

used for the study of the heart's normal behavior and to provide a method for diagnosing abnormalities.

6. Odometer. The device generally shares a housing with the
vehicle's speedometer and is driven by a cable that the two
share.

7. Sextant. The measurement can then be used to determine the
observer's geographical position (latitude or longitude) or
for other navigational, surveying, or astronomical applica-
tions.

8. Galvanometer. When an electric current passes through the
conductor, a magnetic needle tends to turn at right angles to
the conductor so that its direction is parallel to the lines of
induction around the conductor and its north pole points in
the direction in which these lines of induction flow.

9. Sonar. The term is an acronym for sound navigation ranging.

10. Oscilloscope. Displays of such nonelectrical phenomena as
the variations in a sound's intensity can be made if the phenomena are converted into electrical signals.

COMPOSITES

1. Milk fat and solids, a sweetener, flavoring, a stabilizer (usually gelatin), and additions such as eggs, fruits, and nuts.

2. Clay. Brick is made by pressing clay into blocks and firing
them to the requisite hardness in a kiln.

3. Fine rock material, humus, air, and water. The rock material
has been disintegrated by geological changes such as glacia-
tion and volcanic eruption, and humus is the organic
remains of decomposed vegetation. Soil may be from a few
inches to several feet thick.

4. Graphite and clay. The more clay the harder the pencil. Pencils—rods of graphite encased in wood—came into use in the
sixteenth century. The graphite-clay mixture came into use
in the late eighteenth century.

5. Saltpeter (75 percent), sulfur (10 percent), and carbon (15
percent) in the form of charcoal. Gunpowder was the only
explosive in wide use until the middle of the nineteenth century, when it was superseded by nitroglycerine-based explosives.

6. Mohair. The fabric is cool, firm, and resistant to dust and moisture.
7. Brass. Copper constitutes between 55 and 90 percent, zinc the rest. It can be forged or hammered into various shapes, rolled into thin sheets, drawn into wires, and machined and cast.
8. Cement. Once it is mixed with water, cement will harden even if immersed in water.
9. Glass. The silica is obtained from beds of fine sand or from pulverized sandstone. The alkali (needed to lower the melting point of the mixture) is usually a form of soda or potash. Lime acts as a stabilizer. Cullet helps melt the mixture. Other substances may be added to impart such qualities as brilliance, thermal and electrical resistance, and color.
10. Beer. It is one of the oldest of alcoholic beverages, being well known in ancient Egypt.

EVENTS

1. A series of scandals that eventually led to the resignation of President Richard Nixon. In July 1972 agents of Nixon's reelection committee were arrested in Democratic party headquarters in the Watergate apartment building in Washington, D.C., after an attempt to tap telephones there. Subsequent revelations of a high-level conspiracy and cover up forced Nixon to resign.
2. A protest against the British tea tax and import restrictions on the night of December 16, 1773. A group of colonists (led by Samuel Adams, Paul Revere, and others, disguising themselves as Native Americans) boarded three British ships and threw the ships' cargo of tea into the harbor.
3. A series of air battles over Britain in 1940. Germany lost about 2,300 airplanes, Britain about 900. The Battle of Britain was the first major failure of the Germans in World War II.
4. The loosely organized secret network in the United States before the Civil War that helped fugitive slaves reach areas of safety in the free states or Canada.
5. The collaborationist regime set up in Vichy, France, in 1940 by Marshall Henri Pétain after the German-French armistice

of June 22. It controlled unoccupied France and its colonies and became a German tool for the rest of World War II.

6. **The Cultural Revolution.** The army and young revolutionary Red Guards attacked so-called bourgeois elements in cultural circles and in the bureaucracy.

7. **The Bay of Pigs.** In April 1961 about fifteen hundred Cuban exiles, trained by the CIA and supplied with U.S. arms, landed at the Bay of Pigs in Cuba. Most were killed or captured.

8. **The Boxer Uprising (or, Boxer Rebellion).** In June 1900 some 140,000 members of the antiforeign Boxer society occupied Peking and besieged Westerners and Chinese Christians there. The uprising was ended in August by an international force.

9. **The Long March.** Some 90,000 men and women escaped from Nationalist forces in Jiangxi province and undertook the march, led by Mao Zedong. They marched about six thousand miles to Shensi province, losing more than 45,000 people in the one-year trek.

10. **The Crusades.** They took their name from the crosses distributed at the Council of Clermont (1095) at which Pope Urban II exhorted Christendom to war.

INITIALS

1. **The Central Intelligence Agency.** This U.S. agency was established in 1947 by the National Security Act. CIA also stands for "certified internal auditor."

2. **The Internal Revenue Service.** It is a division of the U.S. Department of the Treasury and was established in 1862.

3. **The International Monetary Fund.** A specialized agency of the United Nations, it was established in 1945 (along with the World Bank) as a result of the Bretton Woods Conference in July 1944 and began operations in 1947.

4. **The United Nations Educational, Scientific, and Cultural Organization.** A specialized agency of the United Nations established in 1946, with headquarters in Paris, its goal is to advance the human rights and freedoms laid down in the UN charter through programs of international activities in education, science, and culture.

5. Acquired Immune Deficiency Syndrome. This incurable and fatal disease, identified in 1981, is caused by two retroviruses known as HIV (human immunodeficiency viruses), which attack the immune system and leave the victim vulnerable to infections, malignancies, and neurological disorders. The incidence of AIDS is doubling each year.

6. The National Organization for Women. Founded in 1966 by Betty Friedan, the group seeks to establish full equality for women in America. NOW also stands for "negotiable order of withdrawal."

7. The Palestine Liberation Organization. The coordinating council for Palestine refugee groups, recognized in 1974 by the UN and the Arab states as the government of the Palestinians, was founded in 1964.

8. The Organization of Petroleum Exporting Countries. The members of the organization, established in 1960, are Algeria, Ecuador, Gabon, Indonesia, Iran, Iraq, Kuwait, Libya, Nigeria, Qatar, Saudi Arabia, United Arab Emirates, and Venezuela.

9. The Strategic Defense Initiative. This controversial defense program (popularly called "Star Wars") was announced in 1983 by President Ronald Reagan and continued to be funded under the administration of President George Bush.

10. The American Federation of Labor and Congress of Industrial Organizations. It is a federation of autonomous trade unions in the United States, Canada, Mexico, Panama, and U.S. territories, formed in 1955 by the merger of the AFL and the CIO.

SPORTS AND GAMES

1. American football. In 1966 a merger between the National Football League and the American Football League was negotiated, and the first Super Bowl game was held in January 1967 between the NFL and AFL champions. Four years later the leagues were merged into the present NFL.

2. Baseball. Doubleday (1819–93) was a Union general in the American Civil War. The A. G. Mills commission (1905–1908) reported that Doubleday invented the game at Cooperstown, N.Y., where the National Baseball Hall of Fame and

Museum now stands. Critics point out that a children's game similar to baseball had been played long before Doubleday's time.

3. Ice hockey. Teams hit the disk, called a puck, with sticks whose weight, size, and shape are standardized.

4. Automobile racing. The Indianapolis Motor Speedway is the site of an annual 500-mile automobile race.

5. Chess. Many of the moves in the game are named for the great players who originated them or for countries.

6. Dr. James Naismith. The physical education instructor invented basketball at the YMCA college in Springfield, Massachusetts, in 1891.

7. Scotland banned the game in 1457 because it was a threat to archery practice, considered vital to national defense.

8. It is an abbreviation of "association football." By 1175, what is now known as soccer but was then called football had already been played for centuries in England. In 1823 the advent of rugby football, in which the ball can be handled, led to a confusion of names. When the London Football Association was formed in 1863 to further the game that emphasized only the kicking of the ball, the name was changed to "soccer."

9. England and Australia, in cricket's most famous annual international match. After Australia's surprising victory in 1882, London's *Sporting Times* displayed an obituary for British cricket whose final lines read: "The body will be cremated, and the ashes taken to Australia."

10. The Marquis of Queensberry (1844–1900), the British nobleman, drafted the rules for glove boxing in 1865, which by 1889 were standardized in Britain and the United States. The liaison between Queensberry's son, Lord Alfred Douglas, and Oscar Wilde led to Wilde's notorious trial and subsequent conviction for immoral conduct (homosexuality).

TERMS AND IDEAS

1. A controversial Freudian term designating attraction on the part of the child toward the parent of the opposite sex and rivalry and hostility toward the parent of its own sex.

2. The sweeping progressive reform program of the administration of President Franklin Delano Roosevelt in response to the Great Depression. The term "New Deal" was first used by Roosevelt in his speech accepting the Democratic party's nomination for president in 1932.

3. A writ (literally, "you should have the body" in Latin) directed by a judge to some person who is detaining another, commanding him or her to bring the body of the person in his or her custody at a specified time to a specified place for a specified purpose. It has come to be regarded as the great writ of liberty.

4. The system of statutes (named after a minstrel song) enacted by Southern states and municipalities, beginning in the 1880s, that legalized segregation between blacks and whites. Supreme Court rulings in the mid-1950s began to overturn this legislation.

5. The fervently proclaimed notion that the continental expansion of the United States west to the Pacific Ocean in the 1840s was meant to be the country's almost divinely sanctioned future—its manifest destiny.

6. The Great Society. The 89th Congress (1965–66) enacted more legislative programs than at any time since the New Deal.

7. The Diaspora. The term had originally been used (and is still used) to designate the dispersal of the Jews at the time of the destruction of the Temple and the forced exile to Babylonia.

8. The Monroe Doctrine. President James Monroe (1758–1831), fifth president (1817–25), announced the dual principle of no colonization and no intervention by European states in both hemispheres of the Americas.

9. Home Rule. A basic theme in the history of Ireland through the centuries of English dominance was the desire for control over its own domestic affairs.

10. The Red Shift. The increase is observed in the shifting of individual lines in the spectrum of the object toward the red, or longer wavelength, end of the visible spectrum.

PROCESSES

1. The development from egg to adult in which there is a series

of distinct stages. Examples of metamorphosis are from larva to pupa to adult bee or butterfly, and from tadpole to frog.

2. The accentuation of a beat that would normally be weak according to the rhythmic division of the measure. It is the principal element in ragtime, and in rock music.

3. Uniting parts of two plants so that they grow as one. It is used principally to propagate hybrid plants that do not bear seeds, or plants that do not grow true from seed.

4. The transfer of a liquid solvent through a semipermeable membrane that does not allow dissolved solids to pass. In plants osmosis is at least partially responsible for the absorption of soil water by root hairs and for the elevation of the liquid to the plants' leaves.

5. The use of obstructionist tactics. It has particular reference to unlimited debate in the U.S. Senate.

6. Photosynthesis. Some plants that lack chlorophyll (e.g., the fungi) secure their nutrients from organic material, as do animals.

7. Acupuncture. It is often used as an anesthetic during childbirth and some types of surgery. The patient stays fully conscious throughout, and there is no postoperative hangover or nausea.

8. Taxidermy. The process is employed mainly by museums of science.

9. Metabolism. Exercise, food, and environmental conditions influence metabolism.

10. Exorcism. The practice occurs both in primitive societies and in the religions of more sophisticated cultures.

CONDITIONS

1. The practice, among certain animals, of spending part of the cold season in a more or less dormant state. Animals hibernate to protect themselves against cold when a normal body temperature cannot be maintained and food is scarce. They store food in their bodies, and their body activities decrease to a minimum.

2. The transitional phase in a woman's life when menstruation ceases. The process—the result of declining function of the

ovaries due to their aging—is usually a gradual one. Sometimes it is accompanied by nervousness, flushes, excitability or depression, dizziness, headaches, sweating, and other symptoms.
3. The habitual living together of organisms of different species (usually to their mutual benefit). Examples are the yucca plant and the yucca moth, and the fig tree and the fig moth: in each case, the insect fertilizes the plant, and the plant supplies food for the larvae of the insect.
4. The state after death in which the soul destined for heaven is purified. The suffering is different from that of hell, for the soul in purgatory knows that punishment is temporary.
5. Rapid eye movement sleep (the second stage of sleep), during which the sleeper is deeply asleep but parts of the nervous system are very active and rapid eye movements occur. Sleepers usually dream in this stage of sleep.
6. Coma. The condition may be caused by severe head injury, apoplexy, diabetes, poisoning with morphine or barbiturates, shock, or hemorrhage.
7. Inflation. It results from an increase in the amount of circulating currency beyond the needs of trade. An oversupply of currency leads to an increase in the price of goods and services.
8. Paranoia. In psychology, the paranoid response is the defense mechanism of projection carried to excess.
9. Nirvana. The word in Sanskrit refers to a flame's flickering out once its fuel has been consumed.
10. Syzygy. For example, the moon is in syzygy with the earth and the sun when it is new or full, or when there is a lunar or solar eclipse.

FIELDS AND DISCIPLINES

1. The branch of medicine specializing in the care of children and the treatment of childhood diseases.
2. The study of the relationship between words and meanings. The empirical study of word meanings in existing languages is a branch of linguistics; the abstract study of meaning in relation to language or symbolic logic systems is a branch of philosophy. Both are called semantics.

3. The study of the origin and functioning of humans and their cultures, usually considered a branch of cultural anthropology.

4. The study of animal behavior, especially its physiological, ecological, and evolutionary aspects.

5. The study of the physical and psychological relationship between machines and the people who use them. The design of automobile interiors is an ergonomic exercise.

6. Geriatrics. It is one of the fields included in the general study of old age, or gerontology, which covers psychological, social, and economic factors as well.

7. Ecology. The basic ecological unit is the ecosystem, which may be as small as a tidal pool or a rotting log or as large as an ocean or a continent-spanning forest.

8. Paleontology. Although paleontology deals with early forms of life, it is usually treated as a branch of geology rather than of biology, as the environment of the animals and plants with which it deals cannot be properly understood and reconstructed without knowledge of the age, structure, and composition of the rocks in which their remains are found.

9. Epistemology. It is conventionally distinguished from logic, which is concerned with methods of treating data and with processes and operations of the mind in establishing knowledge.

10. Topology. Once known as analysis situs, it is sometimes referred to as "rubber-sheet geometry" because a figure can be changed to an equivalent figure by bending, stretching, twisting, and the like, but not by tearing or cutting.

DIFFERENCES

1. Arteries carry blood from the heart; veins carry blood back to the heart.

2. Bacteria are microscopic unicellular organisms in one of three typical forms: rod-shaped, round, or spiral. Viruses are organisms composed mainly of nucleic acid within a protein coat and are visible only with an electron microscope. In one stage of their life cycle, when they are free and infectious,

viruses do not carry out the functions of other living cells, such as respiration and growth; however, in the other stage they enter a living plant, animal, or bacterial cell and use its chemical energy and protein- and nucleic acid-synthesizing ability to replicate themselves.

3. Etymology is the branch of linguistics that investigates the origin and development of words. Entomology is the study of insects.

4. In logic, induction is the process of reasoning from the particular to the general. Deduction is the process of reasoning from the general to the particular.

5. Ontogeny is the development of an animal's embryo; phylogeny is the evolutionary development of an animal's ancestors.

6. In flowers, the pistil is the female, the stamen the male reproductive organ. The other two of the four basic parts of a flower are the sepal and the petal.

7. Stalactites grow down from the ceilings of caves; stalagmites grow up from the floors.

8. Meiosis halves the chromosomes when a cell divides; mitosis replicates them.

9. When a ship's sides alternately move up and down, it is rolling; when its front and back alternately move up and down, it is pitching.

10. Tendons attach muscle to bone; ligaments attach bone to bone or bone to cartilage.

PARTS OF THE BODY

1. They separate urea, mineral salts, toxins, and other waste products from the blood. At least one kidney must function properly for life to be maintained.

2. It filters foreign organisms that infect the bloodstream, and also filters out old red blood cells from the bloodstream and decomposes them.

3. It is the chief muscle used in respiration. It acts as a partition between the cavity of the chest and that of the abdomen.

4. It stores and concentrates bile, which functions in the duodenum in the process of fat digestion.

5. It connects the tendons of the calf muscles to the heelbone. It is the strongest and toughest of the human tendons.
6. The fallopian tubes. Fertilization of the ovum usually takes place in the fallopian tube.
7. The pancreas. Pancreatic juice flows into the duodenum through a common duct along with bile from the liver.
8. The iris. It is the area of the eye that is colored, usually brown or blue.
9. Patella. The saucer-shaped bone at the front of the knee joint, it protects the ends of the femur (or thighbone) and the tibia, the large bone of the foreleg.
10. The prostate gland. It is probable that prostatic fluid enhances fertility since the fluid flowing from the testes and seminal vesicles is acidic and sperm are not optimally mobile unless their medium is relatively alkaline.

VEHICLES

1. The ship that brought the Pilgrims from England to New England in 1620. They settled at what is now Plymouth, Massachusetts, on December 26. A replica (the *Mayflower II*) can be seen there today.
2. The flagship commanded by Columbus when he sailed from Spain on August 3, 1492, accompanied by the *Niña* and the *Pinta*. After his historic landing on October 12, Columbus eventually reached Hispaniola on December 5, where the *Santa María* was wrecked on Christmas Eve.
3. The British liner that sank on the night of April 14–15, 1912, after hitting an iceberg in the North Atlantic south of Newfoundland. More than fifteen hundred lives were lost.
4. The spacecraft used for humankind's first moon landing, on July 20, 1969.
5. The airplane in which Charles A. Lindbergh (1902–74) made the first solo nonstop transatlantic flight, from New York to Paris, in 1927.
6. *Sputnik I*. It was launched by the USSR on October 4, 1957.
7. *Challenger*. It exploded seventy-three seconds into its flight, killing all seven crew members, including a civilian schoolteacher, Christa McAuliffe.

8. *Hindenburg.* All aboard the airship were killed. The disaster took place in Lakehurst, New Jersey.

9. *Kon Tiki.* Heyerdahl undertook the crossing with five companions to support his thesis that the first settlers of Polynesia were of South American origin.

10. *Tom Thumb.*This, one of the first U.S. steam locomotives, introduced steam power to the Baltimore and Ohio Railroad. Cooper went on to head North American Telegraph Co., which controlled more than half the telegraph lines in the United States. He founded Cooper Union in 1859, a free institution of higher learning and a pioneer evening engineering and art school in New York City.

FEATURES OF LANGUAGE

1. A figure of speech in which one class of things is referred to as though it belonged to another class, either explicitly (as in Shakespeare's line from *As You Like It:* "All the world's a stage") or implicitly (as in Shakespeare's description of old age as autumn in Sonnet X):

> *That time of year thou may'st in me behold*
> *Where yellow leaves, or none, or few, do hang*
> *Upon those boughs which shake against the cold,*
> *Bare ruined choirs, where once the sweet birds sang.*

2. A figure of speech in which an object is explicitly compared to another, as in Robert Burns's poem "A Red Red Rose":

> *My love is like a red, red rose*
> *That's newly sprung in June:*
> *My love is like the melody*
> *That's sweetly played in tune.*

3. A statement that appears self-contradictory but actually has a basis in truth, such as Oscar Wilde's "Ignorance is like a delicate fruit; touch it and the bloom is gone."

4. A short, polished, pithy saying, often in verse, often with a satiric or paradoxical twist at the end, such as Oscar Wilde's "I can resist everything except temptation."

5. A figure of speech in which exceptional exaggeration is deliberately used for emphasis rather than deception. Andrew Marvell employed hyperbole throughout "To His Coy Mistress":

An hundred years should go to praise
Thine eyes and on thy forhead gaze;
Two hundred to adore each breast;
But thirty thousand to the rest . . .

6. Punning. An example of a pun is Thomas Hood's "They went and told the sexton, and the sexton tolled the bell."
7. An epitaph. Ben Jonson's was brief: "O rare Ben Jonson!" The following is amusing by design or by accident:
   Here lie I Martin Elginbrodde:
   Have mercy on my soul, Lord God,
   As I wad do, were I lord God,
   And ye were Martin Elginbrodde.
8. An acrostic. Early Christians often used a fish as a symbol for Jesus because the Greek word for fish, *ichthus*, was an acrostic: *Iesous Christos Theou Uios Soter* [Jesus Christ God's Son Savior].
9. Irony. In Shakespeare's *Julius Caesar*, when Mark Antony refers in his funeral oration to Brutus and his fellow assassins as "honorable men" he is being heavily ironic.
10. A synonym. Some words are alike in some meanings only, such as *live* and *dwell*.

NUTRITIONAL ELEMENTS

1. A unit of heat energy. In dietetics, one kilocalorie (usually called one calorie) in a food will yield enough heat energy as it passes through the body to raise the temperature of one gram of pure water one degree.
2. Any of the group of highly complex organic compounds found in all living cells and comprising the most abundant class of all biological molecules. Protein comprises approximately 50 percent of cellular dry weight.
3. A fatty substance found in the body tissues of vertebrates. The fact that it is almost insoluble in water is a factor in the development of arteriosclerosis.
4. Chemical compounds including sugars, starches, cellulose, and related compounds that supply energy and produce fats.
5. Saturated fats are generally solid at room temperature, unsaturated fats liquid. Medical research indicates the possi

bility that saturated fats in the diet contribute to the incidence of arteriosclerosis.

6. Grains, fruits, vegetables, meat products, and dairy products. The U.S. Department of Agriculture illustrates a well-balanced diet with the Food Guide Pyramid (1992) showing these groups. Fats, oils, and sweets are at the apex of the pyramid, but are not considered a food group and should be consumed sparingly.

7. The generally indigestible bulky part of food deriving most frequently from plants. Also known as bulk or roughage, fiber has little nutritional value but definite health benefits, particularly in relation to digestion. Foods high in fiber include legumes, green leafy vegetables, fruits, bran, and sprouted seeds.

8. Salt, or sodium chloride. It is widely used as a seasoning and in curing meats and preserving fish and other foods. People with hypertensive heart disease often must restrict the amount of salt in their diet.

9. Vitamin C. Good sources of this vitamin are citrus fruits, red peppers. tomatoes, berries, fresh green vegetables, and potatoes. All animals except humans, other primates, and guinea pigs are able to synthesize ascorbic acid.

10. Vitamin A. Carotene is a pigment present in leafy green vegetables and in yellow fruits and vegetables such as peaches, squash, sweet potatoes, carrots, and corn.

HOLIDAYS

1. July 4th. Celebration of the adoption of the Declaration of Independence on this day in 1776 began during the American Revolution.
2. November 11th. Originally set aside to commemorate the armistice for World War I on November 11, 1918, the day now honors all those who have fought in war for the United States.
3. The first Monday in September. Labor Day was made a national holiday in 1894. The day honoring laborers in most other countries is May 1st (May Day).
4. The fourth Thursday in November. Made an official U.S. holiday in 1863, it traditionally commemorates the harvest reaped by the Plymouth Colony in 1621, after a winter of great starvation and privation.
5. The third Monday in January. King (who was born on January 20, 1929) was shot and killed on April 4, 1968, in Memphis, Tennessee. James Earl Ray was convicted of his murder.
6. Memorial Day. It was initially inaugurated to decorate the graves of Civil War veterans but has since become a day on which all U.S. war dead are commemorated.
7. Christmas (or, the birth of Jesus). The observance of Jesus Christ's nativity probably does not date from before A.D. 200 and did not become widespread until the fourth century.
8. Yom Kippur. It is the most sacred Hebrew holy day, a day of prayer for forgiveness for sins committed during the year.
9. Ramadan. Indulgence of any sort is forbidden during the fast, which commemorates the revelation of the Koran to Muhammad.
10. Practical jokes (or those who fall for them, i.e., "fools"). The English gave April Fool's Day its first widespread celebration during the eighteenth century.

SPORTS EVENTS

1. 1938. The German boxer Max Schmeling had been the only man to defeat Louis (by a twelve-round knockout in 1936). Joe Louis (1914–81) had his revenge two years later with a knockout in the first round.
2. 1973. The one-time-only special tennis match between Billie Jean King and Bobbie Riggs was a well-publicized "battle of the sexes."
3. 1947. Jack Roosevelt "Jackie" Robinson (1919–72) was the first African-American baseball player to play in the major leagues.
4. 1955. As the Los Angeles Dodgers, the baseball team won the World Series in 1959, 1963, and 1965.
5. Between 1967 and 1973. UCLA also had over sixty consecutive victories in regular competition.
6. Jesse Owens. Owens (1913–80) upset Hitler's "Aryan" theories by equaling the world mark (10.3 sec) in the 100-meter race, by breaking world records in the 200-meter race (20.7 sec) and in the broad jump (26 ft, 5 ⅜ in), and by winning (along with Ralph Metcalfe, another African-American athlete) the 400-meter relay race. His records lasted for more than twenty years.
7. Jack Nicklaus (b. 1940). The year 1962 was Nicklaus's first as a professional. He won the Masters six times and the U.S. Open four times.
8. The "Black Sox" scandal. Eight Chicago White Sox players were charged with bribery when it was discovered they had thrown the World Series.
9. Bobby Fischer (b. 1943). He was the first American to win the world championship since the matches started in 1948. Fischer did not play a single game of chess in public for twenty years after his match with Spassky in 1972. In 1992 he was indicted for playing a commercial match in Serbia, against which the United States had an economic boycott.
10. Mark Spitz (b. 1950). He set world records in the 100- and 200-meter freestyle races. He also helped the United States win two gold medals in 1968 and three in 1972.

HUMAN RIGHTS

1. The 1920s. The Nineteenth Amendment to the Constitution granted nationwide suffrage to women in 1920.
2. The 1950s. The Supreme Court unanimously held in 1954 that de jure racial segregation in the public schools was unconstitutional.
3. The 1790s. The Bill of Rights, consisting of the first nine amendments to the Constitution, was added in 1791 to provide adequate guarantees of individual liberties. The tenth amendment, the foundation of states' rights doctrine, was also added in 1791.
4. The 1950s. McCarthyism refers to the indiscriminate attacks by Sen. Joseph McCarthy (R–Wis.) on people he considered Communists and subversives. Through the use of sensationalized tactics, unidentified informers, and unsubstantiated accusations, he ruined the lives and careers of many innocent people on the flimsiest of evidence. He was censured by the U.S. Senate in late 1954.
5. The 1690s. At Salem, Massachusetts, in 1692, twenty people were executed as witches.
6. *Roe v. Wade.* By the 1970s, abortion had been legalized in most European countries, the USSR, and Japan.
7. Rosa Parks. Her action led to a local bus boycott that inspired civil rights activists nationwide.
8. John T. Scopes. He was defended by Clarence Darrow. The prosecutor was William Jennings Bryan. Scopes was convicted but released on a technicality. The Tennessee law was repealed in 1967.
9. Seneca Falls, New York. At the convention Elizabeth Cady Stanton, Lucretia Mott, and other women issued a declaration of independence for women, demanding full legal equality, full educational and commercial opportunities, equal compensation and the right to collect wages, and the right to vote.
10. The Thirteenth. The amendment abolished and prohibited slavery.

MOVIES

1. The 1920s. Spoken dialogue was first successfully introduced into movies in *The Jazz Singer* (1927) with Al Jolson.

2. The 1970s. Steven Spielberg's *Jaws* (1975) unexpectedly grossed over $100 million. His *E.T. The Extra-Terrestrial* (1982) grossed $300 million.

3. The 1960s. Alfred Hitchcock's great suspense movies span five decades, but two of his most terrifying, *Psycho* (1960) and *The Birds* (1963), appeared in this decade.

4. The 1920s. Actor-director Charlie Chaplin's wistful tramp with derby, moustache, baggy trousers, and awkward walk appeared in this decade in *The Kid* (1921), *The Gold Rush* (1925), and *The Circus* (1928).

5. The 1970s. This decade saw a revitalized German film industry, with a world audience for the movies of Werner Herzog (*Aguirre*), Wim Winders (*Kings of the Road*), and R. W. Fassbinder (*The Marriage of Maria Braun*).

6. The 1940s. Humphrey Bogart had outstanding roles in the 1940s in *The Maltese Falcon*, *Casablanca*, *To Have and Have Not*, *The Big Sleep*, *Treasure of the Sierra Madre*, and Key Largo.

7. The 1950s. Marlon Brando starred in *On the Waterfront* (1954), as he did in *A Streetcar Named Desire* (1952). Both movies were directed by Elia Kazan.

8. The 1910s. In this silent classic, director D. W. Griffith introduced the fade-in, the fade-out, the long shot, the full shot, the close-up, the moving-camera shot, the flashback, crosscutting, and montage. Although flawed because of its racism, *The Birth of a Nation* (1915) remains a landmark in the history of the cinema.

9. The 1930s. In the musical *Top Hat* (1935), Fred Astaire and Ginger Rogers give scintillating performances of gaiety and virtuosity.

10. The 1900s. Pioneer director Edwin S. Porter, believing that the continuity of shots rather than the shots themselves were of primary significance, developed the principles of editing and parallel construction. With his *Great Train Robbery* (1903), the new era of film began.

EXACT DATES

1. On December 7, 1941 (at 7:55 A.M.local time). While negotiations were going on with Japanese representatives in Washington, Japanese carrier-based planes attacked the bulk of the U.S. Pacific fleet. The next day, the United States declared war on Japan, thus entering World War II.

2. On November 22, 1963 (at 12:30 P.M. local time). President Kennedy was shot while riding in an open car in Dallas, Texas. He died half an hour later.

3. On June 6, 1944. In World War II on this date, soon after midnight, the Allied invasion of the European continent at Normandy, France, began under the command of Gen. Dwight D. Eisenhower.

4. On July 14, 1789. A mob stormed the Bastille (the hated fortress and state prison in Paris), killed its governor, and freed its inmates. The date is the national holiday of republican France.

5. The night of November 9–10, 1938, became known as Kristallnacht ("the night of glass") because rampaging Nazi brownshirts smashed the windows of Jewish synagogues, shops, and homes throughout Germany and Austria.

6. Julius Caesar was stabbed to death on this day (the Ides of March) in the senate house in Rome.

7. At Hiroshima, Japan, on this day the first atomic bomb ever was dropped on a populated area. About 130,000 people were killed, injured, or missing, and over 90 percent of the city was leveled.

8. This was the day on which humankind—American astronauts Neil A. Armstrong and Edwin E. ("Buzz") Aldrin, Jr.— first walked on the moon.

9. The conquest of Mount Everest. On this day, New Zealand explorer and mountaineer Sir Edmund Hillary and Tenzing Norkay, a Sherpa from Nepal, became the first to reach the summit of the world's highest mountain.

10. On the morning of this day the great San Andreas fault settled violently and San Francisco was shaken by an earthquake which, together with the sweeping three—day fire that followed, all but destroyed the city.

CITY DISASTERS

1. 1990. Kuwait, the city and the country, was devastated by the Iraqi invasion. Over five hundred oil wells were burned, causing phenomenal environmental hazards.

2. 1945. Deaths from the bombing were estimated at between 35,000 and 135,000. Dresden had been ranked as one of the world's most beautiful cities before World War II. Among the city's famous landmarks, all damaged in the war, were the city hall, the Zwinger palace and museum, the Hofkirche (court chapel), and the cathedral.

3. 1975. Most of Phnom Penh's population of 700,000 was driven out of the city and forced to work in the countryside.

4. 1666. The fire lasted five days and virtually destroyed London. Wren built fifty-one churches, including St. Paul's Cathedral.

5. A. D. 64. The fire was attributed (probably falsely) to Nero, who then rebuilt Rome with broader streets and great buildings. Nero accused the Christians of starting the fire and began the first Roman persecution.

6. The Greeks. The events of the final year of the Trojan War as described in the *Iliad* of Homer probably reflect a real war that occurred about 1200 B.C.

7. The German army, in World War II. They slaughtered all but two hundred of the city's half million Jews, and in 1944 expelled the rest of its inhabitants and deliberately demolished the city.

8. Earthquake and fire. More than 150,000 lives were lost in Tokyo that year.

9. Napoleon. The fire served as the signal for an anti-French uprising among the peasants, whose raids, along with the cruel winter, helped to force Napoleon's retreat.

10. The Mongols. The city had been one of the greatest cities of Islam, as reflected in the *Thousand and One Nights*. The Mongol horde destroyed nearly all of its splendor.

BATTLES

1. 1876. At Little Bighorn in southeast Montana, Crazy Horse and Sitting Bull, the Sioux, defeated George Armstrong Custer in the Indian Wars.

2. 1781. The victory at Yorktown of Generals Washington, Rochambeau, Lafayette, and Steuben over General Cornwallis was the closing military operation of the American Revolution.

3. 1836. During the Texas revolution to win independence from Mexico, about 180 volunteer fighters (including Davy Crockett and Jim Bowie) died defending the Alamo in San Antonio against an army of several thousand Mexicans under General Santa Anna.

4. 1863. Gettysburg was the site of the greatest battle of the U.S. Civil War (July 1–3), and later the site of Abraham Lincoln's famous Address on November 19.

5. 1954. At Dien Bien Phu the Viet Minh victory in northwest Vietnam after a 56-day siege marked the end of French power in Indochina.

6. Hastings. The Norman invaders defeated Anglo-Saxon defenders in southeast England in the first and most decisive victory of the Norman conquest.

7. Agincourt. The victory of Henry's longbow men made obsolete the warfare methods of the age of chivalry and enabled England to conquer much of France.

8. The Ardennes in Belgium. The battle, a victorious Allied defense against a German attack penetrating deep into Belgium, lasted from December 16, 1944, to January 16, 1945, and cost the Allies 77,000 casualties.

9. Waterloo. Napoleon signed his second abdication a few days later.

10. Alamein (or El Alamein). The decisive British victory against the Germans saved Egypt for the Allies and led to the defeat of the Axis powers in North Africa.

BOOKS

1. The 1960s. *The Feminine Mystique* (1963) galvanized the

women's movement by attacking the traditional notion that women find fulfillment exclusively through childbearing and homemaking. Friedan founded the National Organization for Women (1966) and helped organize the National Women's Political Caucus (1970).

2. The 1960s. The book (1968) describes the research on the molecular structure of DNA (a "double helix"), for which Watson shared the 1962 Nobel Prize for Physiology or Medicine with colleagues F. H. C. Crick and M. H. F. Wilkins.

3. The 1960s. *Silent Spring* (1962) is a provocative study of the dangers of the use of insecticides.

4. The 1920s. *Three Guineas* (1938) is another feminist work by Woolf. Woolf suffered mental breakdowns in 1895 and 1915; she drowned herself in 1941.

5. The 1940s. *The Second Sex* (1949–50; translated into English in 1950) is a profound analysis of the status of women. Beauvoir was a leading exponent of the existentialist movement and was closely associated with writer Jean-Paul Sartre.

6. Samuel Pepys (1633–1703). His diary (covering the years 1660–69) offers a graphic picture of social life and conditions in the early Restoration period. But because it was written in code, it was not published until the 1890s.

7. Michel Montaigne (1533–92). The first two books of Montaigne's *Essays* were published in 1580, and the first complete edition in 1595. The *Essays*, models of the familiar, digressive style, treat a wide variety of subjects of universal concern and have greatly influenced Western literature.

8. James Boswell (1740–95). Boswell has been called the greatest of all biographers. He first met Samuel Johnson in 1763, eight years after Johnson published his great *Dictionary of the English Language*. Boswell recorded Johnson's conversation so minutely that Johnson is better remembered today for his sayings than for his own literary works.

9. *Walden*. Thoreau's quiet, one-man revolution in living at Walden Pond has become a symbol of a person's willed integrity, inner freedom, and ability to build an individual life.

10. *Democracy in America*. De Tocqueville's work analyzed the American attempt to have liberty and equality in terms of what lessons Europe could learn from American successes and failures.

ART

1. The fifteenth century. Botticelli (c. 1444–1510) was a favorite painter of the Medici family in Florence, where he painted several mythological scenes with allegorical implications.
2. The early sixteenth century. Michelangelo (1475–1564) was commissioned by the city of Florence to execute the magnificent giant *David* for the Piazza della Signoria. It was later moved into the Academy.
3. The early nineteenth century. Goya's terrible and unforgettable etchings were suggested by the Napoleonic invasions of Spain. They constitute an indictment of human evil and a cry of outrage at a world given over to war and corruption.
4. The late fifteenth century. Leonardo's masterpiece of fresco has been badly damaged, but its sublime spiritual content and inventiveness is still powerfully visible.
5. The sixteenth century. Pieter Bruegel the Elder (c. 1525–69) portrayed in vibrant color the living world of field and forest in which lively, robust peasants work and play.
6. The 1870s. Whistler sued art critic John Ruskin in 1878 for writing about this painting that Whistler had asked "two hundred guineas for flinging a pot of paint in the public's face." Whistler won the argument in court, but payment of the court costs left him bankrupt.
7. The 1890s. Rodin's *Thinker* was but one of 186 figures intended, at the appropriate scale, for two great bronze doors never finished, *The Gate of Hell.*
8. The 1890s. Rousseau's fantastic gypsy sleeps in a nighttime desert, closely observed by a lion—the entire absurdity vividly rendered in a compelling, straight-forward manner.
9. The 1860s. Manet's painting of a nude woman with two men in a wood was shown at the Salon des Refuses in Paris in 1863 and was violently attacked.
10. The 1870s. The realism of this painting of a clinic caused a scandal. Eakins's later refusal to abandon the use of nude models forced him to resign his teaching position at the Philadelphia Academy in 1886.

SCIENCE

1. The nineteenth century. Gregor Mendel (1822–84), the Austrian monk and botanist, published his account of his experiments on garden peas in 1866. His work was ignored in his lifetime but was rediscovered by three separate investigators in 1900.

2. The nineteenth century. Dmitri Mendeleev (1834–1907), the Russian chemist, presented his Periodic Law and classified the elements in his Periodic Table in 1869.

3. The seventeenth century. Edmund Halley (1656–1742), the English astronomer and mathematician, saw the comet in 1682 and, identifying it as the same one observed in 1531 and 1607, predicted it would return around 1759. It did. It reappeared most recently in 1986.

4. The twentieth century. Edwin P. Hubble (1889–1953), the American astronomer, presented his law of the uniformly expanding universe in 1929.

5. The seventeenth century. Sir Isaac Newton (1642–1727), the English mathematician and physicist, published *Philosophiae Naturalis Principia Mathematica* (the work's full title) in 1687. It explains how the same phenomenon (gravitation) that affects falling bodies on earth also affects the sun, moon, and planets—indeed, all bodies in space.

6. Werner Karl Heisenberg (1901–1976). The German physicist enunciated his uncertainty principle in 1927. It states that it is impossible to determine both the position and momentum of a subatomic particle (such as the electron) with arbitrarily high accuracy. The effect of this is to convert the laws of physics into statements about relative, instead of absolute, certainties.

7. Max Planck (1858–1947). The German physicist hypothesized in 1900 that oscillating atoms absorb and emit energy only in discrete bundles (quanta) instead of continuously. He received the Nobel Prize for Physics in 1918.

8. Jonas Salk (b. 1914), American physician and microbiologist. Poliomyelitis declined radically in the United States when a mass immunization program was begun in 1955, using the vaccine developed by Dr. Salk.

9. Electromagnetism. James Clerk Maxwell (1831–79), the Scottish physicist, summarized his work in *A Treatise on Electricity and Magnetism* in 1873.
10. The structure of the atom. Lord Rutherford, the British physicist (1871–1937) described the atom in 1911 as a small heavy positively charged nucleus surrounded by negatively charged orbiting electrons.

WOMEN

1. The nineteenth century. Emily Dickinson (1830–86) is considered one of the greatest poets in American literature. Her unique, gemlike lyrics are distillations of profound feeling and original intellect.
2. The sixth century B.C. Sappho was the greatest of the early Greek lyric poets. Her verse is characterized by passion, a love of nature, a direct simplicity, and perfect control of meter. Only fragments survive; the longest (seven stanzas) is an invocation to Aphrodite asking her to help the poet in her relation with a beloved girl.
3. The sixteenth century. Mary Stuart (Mary, Queen of Scots: 1542–87) was beheaded by order of a reluctant Elizabeth I. Mary's reported beauty, charm, and courage in a tempestuous life have made her a particularly romantic figure in history.
4. The fifteenth and sixteenth centuries. The court of Lucrezia Borgia (1480–1519) in Ferrara attracted many artists and poets. Rumors of her participation in her family's poison plots, of incestuous relations with her father and brother, and of her supposed extravagant vices have not been proved.
5. The nineteenth century. George Sand, a pseudonym of the French novelist Amandine Aurore Lucie Dupin, Baroness Dudevant (1804–76), had open and notorious liaisons with Musset, Chopin, and others. She demanded for women the freedom in living that was a matter of course to the men of her day.
6. Catherine II, the Great (1729–96). She made Russia an important country in world affairs, and she was an enthusiastic patron of literature, art, and education. She had many lovers.

7. Amelia Earheart (1898–1937). In 1937 she attempted, with copilot Frederick J. Noonan, to fly around the world, but her plane was lost on the flight between New Guinea and Howland Island.
8. Florence Nightingale (1820–1910). English founder of modern nursing, she was called "The Lady with the Lamp" because she believed that a nurse's care was never ceasing, day or night.
9. Maria Theresa (1717–80). She was also Austrian archduchess and dowager Holy Roman empress. She increased Vienna's reputation as a center of the arts and of music. Among her sixteen children were emperors Joseph II and Leopold II, and Marie Antoinette of France.
10. Murasaki Shikibu (c. 978–1031?). Lady Murasaki was a Japanese court figure, and her novel, *Genji Monogatari*, or *The Tale of Genji*, is ranked with the world's greatest novels. It concerns the life of Prince Genji and his descendants and is a subtle delineation of a complex society.

TECHNOLOGY

1. The twelfth century. Windmills were first used for grinding corn and for pumping water; later they were used for running small sawmills, and later still for driving electrical generators, their main use today.
2. The sixth century B.C. This is the date of the earliest extant horseshoe. The Romans used a leather boot with a metal plate at the bottom as a horseshoe. Before the advent of motor vehicles, horseshoeing was an important trade.
3. The fifteenth or sixteenth centuries. At one time it was generally believed that the first watches had been made in Nuremburg, Germany (c. 1500). However, there is now evidence that watches may have appeared earlier in Italy.
4. The tenth century in China. Canal locks were developed separately in Holland in the thirteenth century.
5. The sixteenth century. The Dutch spectaclemaker Zacharias Janssen is credited with inventing the microscope around 1590. Galileo is also credited with its invention. He announced his invention of the microscope in 1610.

6. The eighteenth century. Around 1765, James Hargreaves invented the spinning jenny, a frame capable of spinning from eight to eleven threads at once. In 1769, Richard Arkwright brought out an improved frame. Very soon, spinning had become a factory enterprise.

7. The 1830s. Samuel Colt invented the revolving-breech pistol.

8. The 1870s. The typewriter, invented by the Americans C. L. Sholes, C. Glidden, and S. Soule in 1867, was manufactured by P. Remington and marketed in 1874. It had only capital letters. A shift-key model appeared in 1878.

9. The 1880s. Quills, plucked from live birds, were used as pens from the Middle Ages until the mid-nineteenth century. Slip-in nibs were in large-scale production in 1828. Ballpoint pens were introduced in the 1940s, felt-tip markers arrived in the 1950s, and fiber-tip markers in the 1960s.

10. The 1920s. Tractors brought profound changes in farm management, displacing not only draught animals but also many farm workers.

JOURNALISM AND THE MEDIA

1. The 1920s. In the United States, the first regularly scheduled broadcasts began in 1920 with the Harding-Cox election returns on KDKA in Pittsburgh.

2. The 1960s. Telstar, the communications satellite, accomplished the first transatlantic television broadcast in 1962.

3. The 1880s. Magazines for women came to dominate magazine circulation by 1900.

4. The 1940s. *Ebony* was directed to an African-American readership.

5. The eighteenth century. Daniel Defoe edited the *Review* (1704–13), Jonathan Swift the *Examiner* (1710–11), Joseph Addison and Richard Steele the *Tatler* (1709–11) and the *Spectator* (1711–12).

6. *Reader's Digest*. The magazine has built a circulation of nearly twenty million and issues many foreign-language editions.

7. The *New Republic*. It was founded in 1909. Like *The Nation*, founded in 1865, it had an influence far exceeding its circu-

lation because its readership comprised intellectuals and public figures.

8. The *National Geographic* magazine was one of the first periodicals to use color photographs.

9. Edward R. Murrow (1908–65). Later a producer and host for many acclaimed television programs such as *See It Now* and *Person to Person*, he also served as director of the U.S. Information Agency from 1961 to 1964.

10. Walter Cronkite (b. 1916). In 1973 a national poll indicated that he was the most trusted newsman in the United States.

ARCHITECTURE

1. In the nineteenth century. The Eiffel Tower in Paris was built in 1889. It is 984 feet high.

2. In the fifth century B.C. The Parthenon, the culminating masterpiece of Greek architecture, was built under Pericles. It stands on the Acropolis at Athens.

3. In the first century A.D. The Colosseum is the most imposing of Roman antiquities. The vast four-storied oval is 617 feet by 512 feet.

4. In the seventeenth century. The Taj Mahal, built in Agra by the Moghul emperor Shah Jahan as a mausoleum for his wife, is the finest example of the late style of Indian Muslim architecture.

5. In the twelfth century. Work on the magnificent cathedral continued into the thirteenth and fourteenth centuries. Notre Dame is a noble achievement of early Gothic architecture in France.

6. The Alhambra. This large group of richly decorated buildings served as a palace-fortress for the Moorish kings. The buildings suffered extensive mutilation when the Moors were expelled from Spain in 1492, but they were restored after 1828.

7. Angkor Watt. Thousands of feet of wall space in this temple complex are covered with impeccably crafted sculptural ornament.

8. Hagia Sophia. This enormous cathedral, now a museum, served as a model for several of the great Turkish mosques of Constantinople.

9. Barcelona. Gaudí (1852–1926), remarkable both for his innovations in technology and for his aesthetic audacity, worked mainly in Barcelona, and the Sagrada Familia is his greatest achievement.
10. Uxmal. This Mayan city, now mostly ruins, contains many fine examples of the late-classical Puuc style.

STYLES AND MOVEMENTS

1. The late nineteenth century. The Impressionists generally tried to depict transitory visual impressions, painted directly from nature, and used broken color to achieve brilliance and luminosity. Monet, Sisley, and Renoir were three originators of the movement.
2. The late eighteenth and early nineteenth centuries. Romantic literature was characterized by belief in a return to nature and the innate goodness of humans; admiration for the heroism, individuality, and imagination of artists; and exaltation of the senses and emotions over reason and intellect. Wordsworth, Coleridge, Shelley, Scott, and Goethe are five of the many great literary Romantics.
3. The seventeenth century. Baroque works in all media were on the grand scale and intensely theatrical. Bernini (1598–1680) was the dominant figure of the Italian Baroque. His *Ecstasy of St. Teresa* in Santa Maria della Vittoria, Rome, is a vital, almost breathing figure.
4. The eighteenth century. In contrast with heavy baroque grandiloquence, rococo was an art of exquisite refinement and linearity. Watteau in France and Tiepolo in Venice exemplified the style.
5. From the mid-twelfth to the sixteenth centuries. Ribbed vaulting, pointed arches, light and soaring spaces, flying buttresses, and pinnacles were typical features of the Gothic style. Chartres Cathedral (twelfth–thirteenth centuries) is an outstanding example of High Gothic.
6. Cubism. Picasso and Braque were the leaders of the movement. Analytical cubism lasted from 1907 till 1912, synthetic cubism (with Juan Gris being the most representative artist) from 1913 through the 1920s.

7. Pop art. Roy Lichtenstein and Andy Warhol were representative artists of the movement.
8. Abstract expressionism. Its leading painters included Jackson Pollock, Willem de Kooning, and Mark Rothko.
9. The Pre-Raphaelites. Their paintings were violently criticized, first by Charles Dickens, as being ugly and vulgar. They were defended by John Ruskin and attracted numerous followers.
10. Art Nouveau. Its themes were symbolic and often erotic. Chief exponents were illustrator Aubrey Beardsley, painter Gustav Klimt, glassware designer Louis C. Tiffany, and architects Antonio Gaudí and Louis Sullivan.

INDEPENDENCE

1. In 1776. On July 4th of that year the Thirteen Colonies fully and formally adopted the Declaration of Independence. The act announced the separation of those colonies from Great Britain and made them into the United States of America.
2. In the 1820s. A Mexican rebellion from 1810 to 1815 failed, but in 1821 Spain accepted Mexican independence.
3. In the 1950s. After Japanese occupation in World War II, Laos became a semiautonomous state in 1949 within the French Union. It received independence in 1953.
4. In the 1940s. The sovereign state of Ireland, or Eire, gained total independence from Great Britain as the Republic of Ireland in 1949 and withdrew from the Commonwealth.
5. In the 1920s and the 1990s. Over four centuries, the Latvian region had been ruled by Poland, Sweden, and Russia. It became independent in 1920 but was forcibly annexed by the USSR in 1940. It became independent again in 1991.
6. Denmark. In 1944 Icelanders voted to end union with Denmark, and on June 17 independence was proclaimed.
7. Portugal. In 1821, Pedro I declared Brazil independent of Portugal and himself emperor. Pedro was the son of John VI, emperor of Portugal.
8. France. In 1962, Algeria became independent of France after more than seven years of bitter fighting.
9. Belgium. The Congo had been since the beginning of the

twentieth century a rich field for European investment, especially in mining operations and plantations. Civil unrest and popular revolt forced Belgium to grant independence in 1960.

10. Holland. In 1945 Sukarno proclaimed an independent Indonesian republic, and in 1949, after intermittent and sometimes heavy fighting, the Dutch finally transferred sovereignty.

WARS

1. 1775–1783. Deteriorating relations between England and its thirteen colonies broke into open conflict on April 19, 1775, near Concord, Massachusetts, with the Battle of Lexington (the first engagement—the "shot heard around the world") and the Battle of Concord on the same day. The American Revolution (also called the American War of Independence and the Revolutionary War) virtually ended with Washington's victory over Cornwallis at Yorktown, Virginia, in 1781, but the Treaty of Paris was not signed until 1783.

2. 1861–1865. The American Civil War between the Northern states (the Union) and the Southern states that had seceded from the Union to form the Confederacy began when Confederate guns, on April 12, 1861, opened fire on Fort Sumter in Charleston (South Carolina) Harbor. The conflict ended on April 9, 1865, with Lee's surrender to Grant at Appomattox Court House in central Virginia.

3. 1914–1918. Although World War I, also known as the Great War, was mainly a war among the European powers, the United States entered the conflict in 1917. Eventually, an armistice came into effect on November 11, 1918 (followed by the signing of the Treaty of Versailles in 1919).

4. 1954–1975. The Vietnam War began soon after the Geneva Conference of 1954 provisionally divided that country into North Vietnam and South Vietnam, leading to civil war. U.S. support for South Vietnam in the early 1960s gradually escalated into a limited international conflict as the United States became more deeply engaged. The war effectively ended with the fall of Saigon in May 1975.

5. 1950–1953. At the end of World War II, Korea had been divided into Soviet (North Korean) and U.S. (South Korean) zones of occupation. In 1950 Chinese forces aided a surprise North Korean invasion of South Korea. UN forces (mostly U.S. and South Korean troops) under Gen. Douglas MacArthur (later replaced by General Ridgway) were sent to South Korea's aid. Negotiations eventually led to an armistice signed on July 27, 1953. A peace treaty has never been signed, and the country remains divided.

6. World War II. Following Germany's invasion of Poland on September 1, 1939, England and France declared war. The conflict would in time involve every major power in the world. The United States entered the war after the Japanese bombed Pearl Harbor on December 7, 1941. Germany surrendered in May 1945, Japan in August 1945.

7. The French Revolution. Only six years after the end of the American Revolution, escalating events in France (notably the storming of the Bastille on July 14 and the abolition of the feudal system on August 4 by the newly formed National Assembly) led to the overthrow of the monarchy and, eventually, to popular sovereignty and democratic rights. The French Revolution lasted until Napoleon Bonaparte's coup d'etat in 1799.

8. The Six Day War. When Egypt closed the Gulf of Aqaba to Israel, Israel responded with air attacks and ground victories. It was in this war that Israel won the Golan Heights, the Gaza Strip, the Sinai Peninsula, the Old City of Jerusalem, and the west bank of the Jordan River.

9. The Russian Revolution. The Revolution of 1905 set the stage for the later February Revolution and October Revolution of 1917, after which Russia was ravaged by civil war between the Reds and the Whites until 1920. These events culminated in the establishment of the Soviet Union (1922), the world's first communist state.

10. The Spanish Civil War. Conservative forces under General Franco overthrew the second Spanish republic. For the youth of the 1930s, saving the republic was the idealistic cause of the era. The war's huge death toll, human suffering, and material devastation was unparalleled in Spanish history.

AGES AND ERAS

1. The fourteenth to sixteenth centuries. Elsewhere in Europe the Renaissance started and ended about fifty years later than in Italy.
2. The sixteenth and seventeenth centuries. The first permanent European settlement in the present United States was St. Augustine, Florida, founded by the Spanish in 1565; the first permanent English settlement was at Jamestown, Virginia, in 1607.
3. The sixteenth century. Beginning as a reform movement within the Roman Catholic Church, the Reformation widened into a much broader religious and political upheaval that ultimately led to the establishment of Protestantism and the freedom of dissent.
4. The fifth to the fifteenth centuries. During this long period in Europe, Christianity was the unifying force of culture, and its ideals were fused with economic, political, and military institutions.
5. The eighteenth century. The Enlightenment, or the Age of Reason, was the mainstream of thought in Europe during this period. Paris was its intellectual center, and Denis Diderot's *Encyclopédie* epitomized its spirit.
6. The nineteenth century. In 1848 the discovery of gold at Sutter's Mill in California brought more than forty thousand prospectors within two years. Other gold rushes took place in Australia (1851–53); Witwatersrand, South Africa (1884); and the Klondike, Canada (1897–98).
7. The mid-fourteenth century. The Black Death started in Constantinople in 1334. In less than twenty years, it is estimated to have killed as much as three quarters of the population of Europe and Asia.
8. From the mid-eighteenth to the mid-nineteenth centuries. In this period of British history dramatic changes in social and economic structures took place as inventions and new technology created the factory system of large-scale machine production and greater economic specialization.
9. The fifth century B. During the time of Pericles (443–429 B.C.) Athenian cultural and imperial achievements reached their height.

10. The seventh to eleventh centuries. Islam started when Muhammad fled Mecca in 622 to become ruler of Medina. The spread of Islam in the eighth century was phenomenal, and the next three centuries were the great period of Muslim thought and culture.

EMPIRES

1. The nineteenth century. The origins of the British empire date from the sixteenth century, but by the end of the nineteenth century the empire included territories on all continents, comprising about one quarter of the world's population and area.
2. The sixteenth century. Almost all of South America, Central America, the southern part of North America, and the Philippines were added to the Spanish world empire.
3. The third quarter of the nineteenth century (or, more precisely, from 1852 to 1870). The first empire was Napoleon's, from 1804 to 1815; the second was his nephew Louis Napoleon Bonaparte's, a period of great prosperity and of colonial expansion, into Senegal and Indochina.
4. The first and second centuries A.D. During these years of peace the Roman empire's boundaries included Armenia, middle Mesopotamia, the Arabian Desert, the Red Sea, Nubia, the Sahara, the Moroccan mountain mass, the Atlantic Ocean, the Rhine, the Danube, the Black Sea, and the Caucasus.
5. The tenth century (or, to be precise, 867–1025). The Byzantine empire lasted from the fourth century until the fifteenth, but between the ninth and the eleventh centuries its eastern frontier was pushed to the Euphrates River, the Bulgars were subjugated, and the Balkan peninsula was recovered.
6. Venice. In the fifteenth century it was the main trading link between Europe and Asia. Its ambassadors, creators of the modern diplomatic service, made the power of the city felt at every court of the known world.
7. The Ottoman. The empire's expansion reached its peak under Selim I (the Terrible) and Sulayman I (the Magnificent) in the sixteenth century. The country controlled Hungary and the countries east of Hungary to the Black Sea; Asia Minor eastwards into Persia and Arabia; Syria; and Egypt.

8. The Netherlands. The superior Dutch vessel, the flute, captured the major share of the world's carrying trade.
9. The Hapsburgs. From 1438 the Holy Roman emperors were, with one exception, Hapsburgs, who controlled central Europe and the Low Countries through marriage. In 1516 Charles V inherited the crown of Spain.
10. The Khmer empire. In the Angkor period (889–1434), the empire extended from the valleys of present-day Thailand to present-day Cambodia and Vietnam and north into Laos.

HUMANITY AND PREHUMANITY

1. The first millennium B.C. Records were kept as soon as writing appeared, but it was not until the time of the Greeks in the first millennium B.C. that historiography emerged.
2. The sixth millennium B.C. Most scholars place the beginning of writing at around 6,000 B.C.
3. The second millennium B.C. Most megalithic monuments in western Europe were erected between 2,000 and 1,500 B.C.
4. The fourteenth millennium B.C. The Lascaux paintings of animals, ascribed to Cro-Magnon man, are drawn with vitality and the elegance of great simplicity. They are the masterworks of prehistoric art.
5. At least five million years ago. The fossil group Ramapithecus is the earliest known representative of the hominid family to which modern humanity belongs.
6. About sixty million years ago. One recent theory suggests that an asteroid impact caused the changes that led to their extinction.
7. Over 350 million years ago. Cockroaches in very much their present form were then extremely abundant on the planet.
8. Between 500 and 700 million years ago. All fauna during that immensely long period of time were marine.
9. Between 4.5 and 5 billion years ago. This estimate is based on radioactive dating of lunar rocks and meteorites, which are thought to have formed at the same time.
10. Between eight and thirteen billion years ago. This is according to the big bang theory favored by most scientists.

CITIES

1. London, England. London's subway went into service in 1863; Boston's in 1898; Paris's in 1900; Berlin's in 1902; New York's in 1904.
2. Munich, Germany. During the games eleven members of the Israeli Olympic team, five Palestinian guerrillas, and a West German policeman were killed in an attack by the guerrillas on the Israeli living quarters in the Olympic village and in a subsequent confrontation at a Munich airport.
3. Yalta, Crimea. The Yalta Conference took place February 4–11, 1945. Among the various decision made there was the decision to divide Germany into four zones of occupation.
4. Potsdam, Germany. The Potsdam Conference took place in July and August of 1945. The leaders agreed to four-power rule over a defeated Germany and discussed reparations payments and the decentralization of Germany's economy. They also issued an ultimatum to Japan.
5. Atlantic City, New Jersey. The city's first boardwalk was built in 1870. The Miss America Pageant is held there every September. After the state legalized casino gambling there in 1976, the city entered a new era of prosperity.
6. Hong Kong. A population of 5,761,500 is packed into an area of 399 square miles. The city is one of the greatest trading and transshipment centers in East Asia.
7. Sydney. The capital of New South Wales, Sydney is Australia's oldest and largest city. Its famous opera house dates from 1973. Sydney's Centerpoint Tower is Australia's tallest building. The capital of Australia is Canberra.
8. Cannes. It is a fashionable resort and seaport on the French Riveria.
9. Florence, Italy. The Medici family directed the destinies of

Florence from the fifteenth century until 1737, making it the golden city, with an incredible flowering of intellectual and artistic life.

10. Vladivostok, on a peninsula between two bays of the Sea of Japan. Russians and Ukrainians comprise most of the city's population.

CAPITALS

1. Sacramento. A deepwater port, it is the shipping, rail, processing, and marketing center for the fertile Sacramento Valley. Aerospace and electronics industries and nearby military installations contribute greatly to the city's economy and development.

2. Ottawa. Founded as Bytown in 1825, it acquired its present name in 1854. The city was selected by Queen Victoria in 1858 as the capital of the newly formed United Provinces of Canada, and began to function as such in 1865.

3. Baghdad. The city's greatest period was under Harun Ar-Rashid in the eighth century, as reflected in the *Thousand and One Nights*.

4. Hanoi. Founded about the seventh century, Hanoi became capital of French Indochina in 1887. It was the capital of North Vietnam from 1954 to 1976, when it became the capital of a united Vietnam once again. The city was bombed heavily by the United States during the Vietnam War, especially in the massive attacks of December 18–30, 1972.

5. Beirut. It was a Phoenician city, and it was prominent under the Seleucids and under Rome. It was captured by the Arabs in 635, and after 1517 it was part of the Ottoman Empire. It became capital of Lebanon in 1920 under the French mandate. Beirut suffered severe damage during the Lebanese civil war (1975–76).

6. Romania. Founded in the fourteenth century, Bucharest became the capital of Walachia in 1648 and of Romania in 1861. It was severely bombed by the Germans in World War II.

7. Alabama. Often called "the cradle of the Confederacy," Montgomery was the site (1861) of the convention that

formed the Confederate States of America. Jefferson Davis was inaugurated as its president on the capital steps.

8. India. New Delhi was built between 1912 and 1929 to replace Calcutta as the capital of India. It was designed by architects Sir Edwin Lutyens and Herbert Baker.

9. Argentina. Buenos Aires was the first Latin American city to revolt (1810) against Spanish rule. Among the city's famous streets is the Avenido 9 de Julio (commemorating Argentina's independence from Spain on July 9, 1816), said to be the world's widest boulevard.

10. Syria. Damascus is reputedly the oldest occupied city in the world. It was inhabited before 2,000 B.C. It has been ruled successively by the Egyptians, the Israelites, the Assyrians, the Persians, Alexander the Great, the Seleucids, the Romans, the Byzantine Christians, the Arabs, the Saracens, the Ottoman Turks, the British, and the French (as part of a League of Nations mandate).

COUNTRIES

1. Brazil. The country occupies nearly half the continent of South America. It was claimed in 1500 by the Portuguese. In 1808, when Portugal's King John VI arrived in Brazil, driven from Portugal by Napoleon, Rio de Janeiro became the capital of the Portuguese empire.

2. The Philippines. Ceded to the United States in 1898 at the end of the Spanish-American War and made an independent republic in 1946, the country is comprised of more than seven thousand islands. Some seventy native languages are spoken there. Tagalog was adopted in 1946 as the basis of a new national language, now known as Filipino.

3. Australia. Domestic rabbits, brought to Australia in 1788, escaped and multiplied so efficiently that by the middle of the nineteenth century they were a menace to sheep raising. In 1907, a 1,000-mile fence was built from the north coast to the south to prevent rabbits from invading Western Australia. But it was the artificially introduced disease myxomatosis that ultimately brought them under control.

4. New Zealand. The country, a consistent world leader in progressive social legislation, gave women the vote in 1893.
5. Ireland. During these years a blight ruined the potato crop, the staple food of Ireland. Hundreds of thousands died from hunger and disease, and many thousands emigrated. Between 1847 and 1854, about 1,600,000 came to the United States.
6. Japan. The islands have many mountains, lakes, rushing rivers, forested slopes, and small rich plains. Mountains cover two thirds of Japan's surface; less than 20 percent of the land is arable, and on the arable sections the population density is among the highest in the world.
7. Venezuela. In 1499 Amerigo Vespucci, in whose honor America is named, came on an island off South America which he nicknamed Venezuela ("little Venice") because of the native villages built above the water on stilts. The name held and was soon applied to the mainland.
8. San Marino, 24 square miles (62 sq km) in the Appenines near the Adriatic Sea, in north central Italy. San Marino also claims to be Europe's oldest existing state. San Marino is the capital, and Serravalle is the only other town.
9. Israel. The state was founded in 1948, and its very existence has been disputed by its neighbors ever since. About 85 percent of its population are Jews, about half of whom are immigrants from Europe, North America, Asia, and North Africa. The non-Jewish population consists mainly of Muslim and Christian Arabs.
10. The eleven states are (from west to east): Alaska, Washington, Idaho, Montana, North Dakota, Minnesota, Michigan, New York, Vermont, New Hampshire, and Maine.

CITY AREAS AND DISTRICTS

1. Los Angeles. Beverly Hills is the home of many film and television personalities.
2. Boston. In the eighteenth and early nineteenth centuries, prominent Boston families built substantial houses on Beacon Hill and in the Back Bay sections of the city and patronized the arts and letters, making the city "the Athens of America."

3. San Francisco. Nob Hill was once the home of millionaires. Other famous areas of the city include Fisherman's Wharf, Chinatown, Telegraph Hill, and Russian Hill.
4. New York City. Early in the twentieth century, "the Village" gained renown as the home of artists, freethinkers, and bohemianism.
5. Venice. The Lido is a long, narrow, sandy island separating the lagoon of Venice from the Adriatic Sea. It has a beautiful beach.
6. The Acropolis. Besides the Parthenon, several of the world's greatest architectural and sculptural monuments are on the Acropolis of Athens.
7. The Loop. This is the downtown section of Chicago, the heart of the city.
8. Montmartre. The highest part of Paris, it was for a long period a favorite residence of the bohemian world. It is famous for its nightlife.
9. The Vatican. Full of architectural and artistic treasures, the Vatican is itself a city, an independent state with the pope its absolute ruler.
10. The Ginza. The business center of Tokyo is the Marunouchi quarter.

STREETS AND BRIDGES

1. San Francisco. The Golden Gate Bridge was opened in 1937. It is one of the world's longest suspension bridges.
2. Florence. The Ponte Vecchio, built in the fourteenth century, was the only bridge in the city to survive World War II.
3. Venice. The Bridge of Sighs leads from the Doge's Palace on St. Mark's Square to the state prison, where prisoners were led directly after trial.
4. New York City. The Great White Way is the theater district section of Broadway, the longest street in the world.
5. Hamburg. The Reeperbahn is in the St. Pauli district of the city, where there are numerous places of entertainment.
6. The Verrazano Narrows Bridge. Built in 1964, this is the longest suspension bridge in the United States (a main span of 4,260 feet).

7. London Bridge. Built in 1831, it was shipped to Arizona in 1968. The old bridge was replaced in London by a six-lane concrete bridge.

8. The Champs Elysées. The avenue is celebrated for its tree-lined beauty, its commodious breadth, the elegance of its cafes, theaters, and shops, and the fountain display at its center.

9. Fleet Street. It is in the district of London known as the City. Other famous streets in London are the Strand, Piccadilly, Whitehall, Pall Mall, Bond Street, and Regent Street.

10. The Kurfurstendamm. The church is located right in the center of the city, and its gutted tower has been left unrestored as a reminder of World War II.

PARKS AND SQUARES

1. London. The city has many squares and parks. The parks include Kensington Gardens, Hyde Park, and Regent's Park.

2. Moscow. During the period of Communist rule, Red Square was the site of demonstrations and huge military parades. St. Basil's Cathedral is at its south end.

3. Beijing. In mid-1989, the square became the focal point for large but peaceful demonstrations for democratic reform in China which were brutally put down by the Chinese military.

4. Venice. St. Mark's Church is on the square, as is the Doge's Palace and the campanile.

5. Washington, D.C. The Tidal Basin is flanked by cherry trees and is itself a section of the large West Potomac Park.

6. Tivoli Gardens. The gardens were opened in 1843. Copenhagen's charm and design have earned it the name "the Paris of the North."

7. The Tuileries. The Tuileries palace, which had stood in the splendid formal gardens, was destroyed by fire in the Commune of Paris in 1871.

8. The Tiergarten. It also contains the Reichstag building and the American-designed Kongress Halle.

9. Wenceslaus Square. It was the center of Czech resistance in the 1968 Soviet invasion of the country.

10. Gethsemane. Ruins of a fourth-century church and of a church as old as the Crusades have been found here.

BUILDINGS

1. Pisa. The marble tower is slightly more than 180 feet high and sixteen feet from the perpendicular.
2. Philadelphia. Independence Hall was the scene of the proclamation of the U.S. Declaration of Independence (1776) and was the meeting place of the Continental Congress and the Constitutional Convention.
3. London. This famous address is the official residence of the Prime Minister of Great Britain. Nearly all prime ministers from the time of Robert Walpole in the eighteenth century have lived there. It was damaged in the bombing of World War II but has been rebuilt.
4. Moscow. The Kremlin is not actually one building, but a fortified complex occupying ninety acres. Surrounded by fifteenth-century crenellated walls topped by twenty towers, the complex encompasses several cathedrals and palaces.
5. San Simeon, California. It was erected from 1919 on and became famous for its huge art collections, which often overflowed into warehouses.
6. The Pentagon, in Arlington, Virginia. Housing the U.S. Department of Defense, the structure comprises five concentric buildings connected by corridors and covers an area of thirty-four acres.
7. The Texas State School Book Depository. Lee Harvey Oswald was held by the Warren Commission to have been the sole assassin.
8. The Tower of London. It has been a royal residence, a jail for illustrious prisoners, and an arsenal. It is now guarded by "Beefeaters."
9. Fallingwater. The building is dramatically cantilevered over a waterfall.
10. Tintern Abbey. It was founded in 1131. The ruins are mainly of thirteenth- and fourteenth-century design.

INSTITUTIONS

1. Paris. It is the foremost French museum of art. The building dates from the sixteenth century, with additions in later centuries.
2. St. Petersburg. The museum houses over 40,000 drawings, 500,000 engravings, and 8,000 paintings of the Flemish, French, Dutch, Spanish, and Italian schools—and this is still only a fraction of the riches in this collection, which was originated by Catherine the Great.
3. Madrid. The national Spanish museum houses countless outstanding works of art.
4. London. Opened in 1897, the gallery is particularly noted for its collection of works by Blake, Turner, and the Pre-Raphaelites.
5. Florence. The Uffizi, once a sixteenth-century palace, now houses one of the greatest collections of art in the world. It is especially strong in Italian Renaissance paintings.
6. The Menninger Clinic, founded in 1920. The clinic and the Menninger Foundation have made Topeka a world-famous center for psychiatric research.
7. The Mayo Clinic, founded in 1899 by the Mayo brothers. In 1915 they established the Mayo Foundation.
8. The International Red Cross. The symbol of a red cross on a white background, a Swiss flag with colors reversed, was chosen to honor the nationality of its founder Jean Henry Dunant (1828–1910).
9. Woods Hole Oceanographic Institution, established in 1930. In addition to oceanographic research, it conducts important work in meteorology, biology, geology, and geophysics.
10. CERN, founded in 1954. The activities of the Centre Européen de la Recherche Nucleaire are sponsored by twelve European countries, and it is the principal European center for research in particle physics.

BIRTH PLACES

1. Russia. Vladimir Nabokov (1899–1977), born in St. Petersburg, wrote his first fiction in Russian but went on to

become one of the most original masters of modern fiction in English.

2. Australia. Rupert Murdoch (b. 1931), the publishing magnate, established an international newspaper, book, magazine, and television empire. He became a U.S. citizen in 1982.

3. The United States. Maria Callas (1923–77), the opera singer born to Greek parents in New York City, was noted for her dramatic intensity, excelling in *Medea, Norma»,* and *Tosca.*

4. India. Salman Rushdie (b. 1947) won acclaim with his novels *Midnight's Children* (1981) and *Shame* (1983). His allegorical novel *The Satanic Verses* (1988) enraged many Muslims, including the Ayatollah Khomeini, who sentenced Rushdie to death. Rushdie went into hiding.

5. Poland. Conrad (1857–1924) acquired English as his second language and in many works of fiction became one of the greatest novelists and prose stylists in English literature.

6. George Balanchine (d. 1983). He moved to the United States in 1933 and as artistic director and choreographer of the New York City Ballet became one of the most important figures in ballet of the twentieth century.

7. Yo-Yo Ma. He studied in New York with Leonard Rose and appeared at Carnegie Hall in 1964.

8. Doris Lessing. She went to England in 1949. In her fiction she has been principally concerned with detailing the lives of intelligent women—their psychology, their work, their relationship to men and to their children, their change of outlook as they age.

9. Marc Chagall (1889–1985). Much of his work is rendered with extraordinary formal inventiveness and a deceptive fairy-tale naïveté.

10. Elie Wiesel (b. 1928). At sixteen he was imprisoned in Nazi concentration camps at Auschwitz and Buchenwald. His writings have focused on the importance of remembering the Holocaust.

DEATH PLACES

1. Paris, France. Edward VIII (1894–1972), known as the Duke of Windsor after he abdicated the throne in 1936, married

Wallace Warfield Simpson (a commoner) and lived outside England. He was buried at Windsor.

2. The Philippines. Ferdinand Magellan (c. 1480–1521), the great Portuguese navigator, was killed there while supporting one group of natives against another. He was leading the world's first circumnavigation, one of the greatest achievements of exploration, and one that definitively proved the roundness of the earth.

3. The Hawaiian Islands. James Cook (1728–79), the English explorer and navigator, was killed by natives on the return journey of a three-year expedition that had included a year in the Pacific.

4. Samoa. Stevenson (1850–94), the Scottish novelist, poet, and essayist, was by his own request buried high on Mt. Vaea "under the wide and starry sky," which he had described in his poem "Requiem."

5. Moscow, Russia. Reed (1887–1920) wrote *Ten Days That Shook the World* (1919), considered the best eyewitness account of the 1917 Russian Revolution. He died of typhus in Moscow and is buried in the Kremlin.

6. Ezra Pound (1885–1972). The American poet, critic, and translator broadcast Fascist propaganda to the United States for the Italians during World War II and was later indicted for treason. After spending twelve years in a mental hospital in Washington, D.C., he returned to Italy.

7. Sylvia Plath (1932–63). The American poet was married to the English poet Ted Hughes. Her best-known work is probably *The Bell Jar* (1963), a semiautobiographical novel.

8. Oscar Wilde (1854–1900). The celebrated Irish author and wit spent two years in jail for homosexual offenses, which resulted in his well-known poem *The Ballad of Reading Gaol* (1898). He lived his last three years in France, ill and bankrupt.

9. James Joyce (1882–1941). He lived on the Continent from 1904, returning to Ireland only briefly. He wrote *Ulysses* between 1914 and 1921. Its publication was banned in the United States until 1933.

10. Dylan Thomas (1914–53). The Welsh poet, known for his *Collected Poems* (1952) and the radio play *Under Milk Wood* (1954), died after reckless drinking during his third popular tour of the United States.

EVENTS

1. Northern Spain. One of Picasso's greatest paintings commemorates the 1937 destruction of the town by German bombers aiding General Franco during the Spanish Civil War.
2. Central India. In December 1984 this city became the site of the worst industrial accident in history when a toxic gas leak form a Union Carbide insecticide plant killed more than 8,000 people and injured approximately 150,000.
3. Alaska. In 1989 an oil tanker bringing oil from Prudhoe Bay spilled ten million gallons of oil in Prince William Sound near the port of Valdez, causing severe economic and environmental damage.
4. Scotland. In December 1988 an airplane exploded in flight as a result of a terrorist bomb and crashed into Lockerbie. All 259 people aboard the plane and eleven on the ground were killed.
5. Ukraine. Chernobyl was the site of the world's worst nuclear accident in April 1986.
6. Kitty Hawk. In 1903, the Wright brothers made the first four controlled, sustained flights in a power-driven airplane there.
7. Maastricht. The treaty was an important step in the continuing integration of the European Community.
8. Los Alamos. In this town the first atomic bombs were produced. In 1947 the Atomic Energy Commission took over the town, and the U.S. government controlled it until 1962.
9. Sarajevo. The assassination precipitated World War I. Sarajevo was under Serbian siege from April 1992.
10. Guyana, in South America. The suicides in the jungle village of Jonestown were members of Rev. Jim Jones's People's Temple cult.

CHANGED NAMES

1. Thailand. Siam was renamed in 1938.
2. Zambia. Northern Rhodesia became independent as Zambia in 1964 with Kenneth Kaunda as its first president.

3. Iran. Persia's name was changed to Iran in 1935 by royal decree.
4. Sri Lanka. Ceylon has been named Sri Lanka since 1972.
5. Myanmar. Burma was renamed in 1989 by its military government to better reflect the nation's ethnic diversity.
6. New Amsterdam. It was a small Dutch settlement on the tip of Manhattan island, which the Dutch had bought for twenty-six dollars' worth of trinkets from its Native American inhabitants. The English seized the colony in 1664 and renamed it New York.
7. Saigon. It was renamed Ho Chi Minh City at the end of the Vietnam War.
8. Yerba Buena. The settlement was renamed San Francisco in 1846, when its population was eight hundred. By 1850 the gold rush had added about twenty thousand people to its population.
9. Petrograd and Leningrad. St. Petersburg, built in 1703, was renamed Petrograd in 1914. Its name was changed again in 1924 to Leningrad. In 1991 its name was changed yet again, back to St. Petersburg.
10. Byzantium and Constantinople. Constantine I ordered a new city built in A.D. 330 on the site of Byzantium. The city, Constantinople, became the capital of the Byzantine empire. It was renamed Istanbul six hundred years later in 1930.

PEOPLES

1. Japan. The samurai were aristocratic knights of feudal Japan. The class arose in the twelfth century and was abolished after the Meiji restoration in 1868.
2. The United States. The Comanche were nomadic plains horsemen whose tribe ranged the southwestern United States from the eighteenth century. They killed more whites in proportion to their numbers than any other Native American peoples. Today some 3,500 live in Oklahoma.
3. Ukraine. The Cossacks were peasant-soldiers in Ukraine and in several regions of the former Russian Empire who received certain privileges in return for their military service. Most fought against the Red Army in the 1918–20 civil war.

Their communities were collectivized (1928–33), but many of their traditions survive.

4. Peru. The advanced and highly organized pre-Columbian Inca empire dominated the entire Andean region of west South America.

5. Ghana. The Ashanti are one of Ghana's major ethnic groups. In the seventeenth century, the Ashanti federation was forged, but after the Anglo-Ashanti wars in the nineteenth century, the federation was dissolved.

6. The Basques. They are probably the oldest ethnic group in Europe. Basque nationalism, often involving violent incidents, has been a feature of recent Spanish politics.

7. The Kurds. The majority are devout Sunni Muslims. Kurdistan, an extensive plateau and mountain region, includes parts of eastern Turkey, northeast Iraq, northwest Iran, northeast Syria, and Armenia.

8. The Inuit. Although they are widely dispersed, they have remained extremely uniform in language (dialects of Eskimo-Aleut), physical type (Mongoloid), and culture.

9. The Lapps. In Norway they are called Samme or Finns. They speak a Finno-Ugric language. Lapland is a vast region of northern Europe, largely within the Arctic Circle.

10. The Maoris. They are believed to have migrated from Polynesia in ancient times. In the nineteenth century, wars against European encroachment reduced their numbers to 100,000. Their numbers later dwindled to 40,000, then gradually increased.

ISLANDS

1. Ellis Island. It is now part of the Statue of Liberty Monument, and the main building has been restored.

2. Alcatraz. It became part of the Golden Gate National Recreation Area in 1972.

3. The Galápagos Islands. They are famous for their wild life, especially for their gigantic land tortoises, land and sea iguanas, and flightless cormorants.

4. The Falkland Islands. They are in the South Atlantic and are a British colony, with a population of about two thousand

people. In 1982 the islands were seized by Argentina but were retaken by British troops.

5. Crete. The Minoan civilization was one of the world's earliest, flourishing about 1600 B.C.
6. Greenland. It is about 840,000 square miles, of which all but 132,000 square miles is covered by an ice sheet. Australia, much larger than Greenland, is considered a continent rather than an island.
7. Mont-Saint-Michel. The island is accessible by land from the mainland at low tide. Its collection of buildings, constructed from 1203 to 1228, is one of the most imposing achievements of Gothic architecture.
8. Krakatau, between Java and Sumatra in Indonesia. The explosion scattered debris across the Indian Ocean as far as Madagascar.
9. The United States. The islands, separating the Bering Sea from the Pacific Ocean, came as part of the purchase of Alaska by the United States in 1867.
10. Madagascar, off the east coast of Africa. The country gained its independence from France in 1960.

MOUNTAINS

1. In Africa. Kilimanjaro, in Tanzania, has two peaks, the higher of which is 19,340 feet, making it that continent's highest mountain.
2. In Asia, ranging through Pakistan, India, China, Nepal, Sikkim, and Tibet. Everest is the highest peak of the Himalayas.
3. East Turkey, near the Iranian and Russian borders. The tradition that Mount Ararat is the resting place of Noah's ark is based on a misreading of Genesis 8.4, which properly reads "upon the mountains of Ararat," indicating a country or region.
4. Between France and Spain. The Pyrenees is a formidable natural barrier between the countries. Its population is largely Basque and Béarnaise. The small republic of Andorra is in the Pyrenees.
5. Between Europe and Asia. The Caucasus extends about 750

miles from the mouth of the Kuban River on the Black Sea southeast to the Apsheron Peninsula on the Caspian Sea. Over forty languages are spoken by the ethnic groups of the entire region.

6. Mount Saint Helens. Its eruption killed sixty-five people, sent a volcanic plume sixty thousand feet into the air, triggered fires and mudslides, and blanketed a large area with ash.

7. Mount Fuji (or Fujiyama). Its last major eruption was in 1707. A sacred mountain and a traditional goal of pilgrimage, it is the highest mountain in Japan.

8. Vesuvius. Its first recorded eruption in A.D. 79 buried Pompeii, Herculaneum, and Stabeae under cinder, ashes, and mud. It has erupted many times since then.

9. Mount Olympus. At about 9,570 feet, it is the highest point in Greece. The peak was first ascended in 1913.

10. Presidents Washington, Jefferson, Lincoln, and Theodore Roosevelt. Carved by sculptor Gutzon Borglum, the 60-foot likenesses are visible from sixty miles. The site is in the Black Hills of South Dakota.

LAKES AND RIVERS

1. In Africa. The Nile, 4,160 miles long, flows through or touches Burundi, Zaire, Rwanda, Uganda, Kenya, Ethiopia, Sudan, and Egypt.

2. Between Europe and Asia. The Caspian Sea is a salt lake and is about 144,000 square miles in area. Variations in the evaporation of its water account for the great changes in its size during the course of history. The northern part is the chief source of Beluga caviar.

3. Between the United States and Canada. Lake Superior is 31,820 square miles in area. It is not only the largest of the Great Lakes but also the highest and the deepest.

4. Between Peru and Bolivia. The largest lake in South America, Lake Titicaca is about 12,500 feet above sea level in the Andes mountains.

5. In Africa. Lake Victoria is the largest freshwater lake in Africa.

6. The Amazon. Its drainage basin is enormous (about 2,500,000 square miles), gathering waters from both hemispheres and covering not only most of north Brazil but also parts of Bolivia, Peru, Ecuador, Colombia, and Venezuela.

7. The Hudson, in New York State. Many painters of the Hudson River School, including Thomas Cole and Frederick Church, found inspiration during the middle of the nineteenth century in the tranquility, grandeur, and wild beauty of this river.

8. The Danube. This great river (about 1,770 miles long) touches the land of Germany, Austria, Czechoslovakia, Hungary, Yugoslavia, Bulgaria, and Romania.

9. The Arno. Many great art treasures were damaged in the flood.

10. Canada. It contains nearly 50 percent of the world's lakes.

OCEANS, SEAS, AND GULFS

1. Between parts of Mexico. Baja California is on the west of the Gulf of California, and the Mexican mainland is on the east.

2. Between Italy on the west, and Slovenia, Croatia, Bosnia and Herzegovina, Yugoslavia, and Albania on the east. Venice is the chief port of the Adriatic.

3. Between China's east coast and Korea. Colored silt, deposited by feeder rivers, gives the Yellow Sea (or Hwang Hai) its name.

4. The Red Sea separates northeast Africa from the Arabian Peninsula. In the north it divides into the Gulfs of Suez and Aqaba. It was probably named for the reddish algae that appear in it at certain times of the year.

5. The Indian Ocean. The Republic of Seychelles consists of approximately eighty-five islands. Sixty-five percent of the population lives on the largest island, Mahe.

6. The Pacific Ocean. It occupies about one third of the earth's surface (about seventy million square miles).

7. The Aegean. The island-studded sea is off southeast Europe between Greece and Turkey.

8. The Atlantic Ocean and the Mediterranean Sea. The Strait of Gibraltar lies between Spain and Morocco.

9. An area in the Atlantic Ocean where a number of ships and aircraft have vanished. It lies between Florida, Bermuda, and Puerto Rico. Storms are common in the area, and investigations to date have not produced evidence of any unusual phenomena involved in the disappearances.
10. Not on earth, but on the moon. The "oceans," "seas," and "lakes" on the moon's surface were thought by early astronomers to be bodies of water, but they are land areas, covered by a thin layer of powdered rock.

AREAS OF THE WORLD

1. North Africa. The Sahara is the world's largest desert, extending about three thousand miles east to west, and about twelve hundred miles north to south.
2. The northern third of Asia, stretching from the Urals in the west to the mountain ranges of the Pacific Ocean watershed in the east, and from arms of the Arctic Ocean in the north to the Mongolian People's Republic in the south.
3. Germany. The Ruhr is the principal manufacturing center of Germany and one of the world's greatest industrial complexes.
4. France, Monaco, and Italy. The French and Italian Rivieras are a continuous narrow coastal strip between the Alps and the Mediterranean, extending, roughly, from Hyères in France to La Spezia in Italy. The French Riviera is also called the Côte d'Azur, and it includes Monte Carlo in Monaco.
5. The Iberian Peninsula, in Southwest Europe, comprises Spain and Portugal.
6. The Netherlands, Belgium, and Luxembourg. The Low Countries are in northwestern Europe.
7. Estonia, Latvia, and Lithuania. They border the eastern coast of the Baltic Sea in northern Europe.
8. Sweden, Norway, Denmark, Finland, and Iceland are the countries of Scandinavia in northern Europe.
9. The Balkan states are Albania, Greece, Bulgaria, European Turkey, Bosnia and Herzegovena, Slovenia, Croatia, Romania, Macedonia, and Yugoslavia. Yugoslavia has since 1992 been a federation of the two republics of Serbia and Mon-

tenegro. The Balkan peninsula is the southeastern most peninsula of Europe.

10. Maine, New Hampshire, Vermont, Massachusetts, Rhode Island, and Connecticut. New England was the center of the many historical events that led to the American Revolution.

THE EARTH, THE WORLD, AND THE CONTINENTS

1. The earth is between the sun and the moon during a lunar eclipse, blocking the sun's light from the moon.
2. The moon.is between the sun and the earth during a solar eclipse, blocking the sun's light from the earth.
3. The equator. The North Pole and South Pole are ninety degrees north and south respectively.
4. Any point on the line running from pole to pole through the original site of the Royal Greenwich Observatory at Greenwich, England. All other points on the earth have longitudes ranging from zero degrees to 180 degrees east or west.
5. Africa. Guinea is bounded on the north by Guinea-Bissau, Senegal, and Mali; on the east by Côte d'Ivoire; on the south by Sierra Leone and Liberia; and on the west by the Atlantic Ocean.
6. Australia. The world's second largest island, New Guinea is situated in the southwest Pacific, north of Australia, from which it is narrowly separated at one point by the Torres Strait.
7. South America. Guyana is bounded on the north by the Atlantic Ocean, on the east by Surinam, on the south by Brazil, and on the west by Venezuela.
8. The northern. In South America, the equator runs through Ecuador, Colombia, and Brazil, south of Venezuela.
9. Australia. It lies between the Indian and Pacific oceans, and with the island state of Tasmania, the continent makes up the Commonwealth of Australia. It is the only continent occupied by a single nation.
10. There is no land at the North Pole, which is in the middle of the Arctic Ocean. The South Pole is in the middle of the Antarctic continent.

FICTIONAL PLACES

1. Camelot. The origin of the name is unknown. It has been variously located in England at Cadbury Camp, Somerset; Winchester; Camelford; and Caerleon.
2. Utopia. Sir Thomas More (1478–1535), the author of *Utopia*, was a man of great personal charm, unfailing good humor, piercing wit, and remarkable fearlessness. He refused to subscribe to Henry VIII's Act of Supremacy, which impugned the pope's authority and made Henry the head of the English church. He was imprisoned in the Tower of London and beheaded.
3. El Dorado ("the Golden Man"). Much of the impetus for Spanish exploration of the New World came from the story of this South American Indian chief and his legendary land of gold and plenty, whose long-sought location seemed to shift as new regions were explored.
4. Middle Earth. British author and Oxford professor J. R. R. Tolkien (1892–1973) set his *Lord of the Rings* trilogy and *The Hobbit* in this mythological kingdom.
5. Brobdingnag. After Lilliput, populated by tiny people, Lemuel Gulliver travels to Brobdingnag, populated by giants. These countries, and other extraordinary places visited by Gulliver, are the creations of Jonathan Swift (1667–1745) in *Gulliver's Travels* (1726).
6. Atlantis. Questions as to its actual existence have provoked speculation over the centuries. One theory holds that it was part of the Aegean island of Thera that sank about 1500 B.C.
7. Valhalla. This martial paradise was one of the most beautiful halls of Asgard, the home of the gods.
8. Yoknapatawpha County, Mississippi. Faulkner (1897–1962) gave his imaginary county a colorful history and richly varied population. He won the Nobel Prize for literature in 1949.
9. Wessex. Thomas Hardy (1840–1928) made the county bleak and forbidding, with a physical harshness echoing that of an indifferent, if not malevolent, universe.
10. Barsetshire. Trollope (1815–82) wrote six novels, including *The Warden* (1855) and *Barchester Towers* (1857), set in this imaginary county.

LENGTH

1. 5,280 feet. There are 1,760 yards in a mile, and three feet in a yard.

2. About twenty-three feet long. The human intestine is a narrow tube winding compactly back and forth within the abdominal cavity from the lower end of the stomach to the anus.

3. One hundred yards. The American football field is 53½ yards wide.

4. 1.609 kilometers. The metric system, planned in France and adopted there in 1799, has been adopted by most of the technologically developed countries of the world.

5. Twenty-nine feet. This is one of the major recent track and field accomplishments.

6. A crocodile can be as long as fourteen feet, whereas an alligator generally reaches nine feet.

7. The distance that flying fish can fly (or, actually, glide)—as much as a quarter mile—is longer. Their velocity in the water builds up to thirty miles per hour as they approach the surface until they launch themselves into the air, vibrating their specially adapted tail fins in order to taxi along the surface. A dolphin's graceful, arched leap reaches thirty feet.

8. The blue whale. It may attain a length of one hundred feet, whereas the ferocious white shark grows to only twenty feet.

9. The longest worm, in the nemertine phylum. It can reach ninety feet. The longest snakes, in the boa family, reach thirty feet.

10. The African bull elephant's tusk, which can reach ten feet, is longest. A walrus's tusk can reach three feet; an African black rhino's horn eighteen inches; and a boar's tusk nine inches.

HEIGHT

1. Eighteen feet (in a full-grown male) from hoof to crown. Its neck, up to seven feet long, has seven vertebrae, like other mammals, but each is very elongated.
2. Ten feet. The basketball hoop's diameter is eighteen inches.
3. Eight feet. This is one of the recent accomplishments of track and field athletics. It is a whole foot higher than had been reached at the time of the last edition of *The Columbia Encyclopedia* (1975).
4. Twenty feet. This height, like the 8-foot high jump, is one of the recent accomplishments of track and field athletics. It has been raised two feet since 1975.
5. 29,028 feet. Everest is called Chomo-Lungma (Mother Goddess of the Land) by the Tibetans. The peak is the highest elevation in the world.
6. The Washington Monument, which is nearly 556 feet high, whereas the California redwood, probably the tallest tree in the world, grows to about 385 feet high.
7. Angel Falls (3,212 feet), in southeast Venezuela, is the world's highest known waterfall. Niagara Falls on the American side is 167 feet high.
8. The broadcasting tower in Toronto, which is the world's tallest structure at 1,821 feet. The Sears Tower is the tallest building in the world, at 1,454 feet.
9. The ozone layer, which is thirty miles above the surface of the earth. The jet stream is seven to eight miles above the surface of the earth. There are two major streams circling the earth eastwards at an average 35 miles per hour in summer and 75 miles per hour in winter. Eastbound air flights are usually faster than westbound ones for this reason.
10. Cirrus clouds are higher. Composed entirely of ice crystals, these are detached clouds of delicate and fibrous appearance, without shading, generally white in color, often resembling tufts or featherlike plumes, and occur between 20,000 and 40,000 feet. Stratus clouds, a uniform layer resembling fog but not resting on the ground, occur at about 3,000 feet.

DEPTH

1. About eight-ninths. Only about one-ninth (the "tip") of an iceberg shows above water.
2. Up to twelve inches. Blubber is an insulating layer of fat under the whale's skin.
3. The Grand Canyon is about one mile deep (thus, 5,000 to 5,300 feet would be correct). Plant life on the Grand Canyon's walls varies from subtropical at the base to subarctic near the rims.
4. About 4,000 (or, to be exact, 3,963 miles). From the poles it is 3,950 miles to the center of the earth. The earth is slightly flattened at the poles and bulging at the equator.
5. About twenty-five miles deep (or thick). According to the theory of plate tectonics, the continents are embedded in large plates that drift about on the earth's surface.
6. The surface of the Dead Sea. At 1,292 feet below sea level, it is the lowest point on earth and supports no life at all (because of its high salt content). Death Valley, 282 feet below sea level, is the lowest point in the Americas.
7. The depth sea lions can dive to, which is six hundred feet. Scuba divers experience nitrogen narcosis ("rapture of the deep") at about 130 feet. It is caused by the narcotic effects of the air's nitrogen at high pressure, resulting in serious and dangerous loss of judgment.
8. The burrows of badgers, which may be thirty feet below ground level. Kingfishers may extend their burrows down ten feet vertically.
9. The depth sperm whales can dive to, which is a mile down. Plants exist under water only to a depth of about three hundred feet, below which there is insufficient light for photosynthesis.
10. The deepest part of the ocean yet discovered is the Challenger Deep of the Mariana Trench in the Pacific Ocean, which reaches maximum known depths of 36,198 feet below sea level. Its bottom was reached in 1960 by two men in a U.S. navy bathyscaphe. The deepest lake in the world is Lake Baykal in southeast Siberia (maximum depth 5,714 feet).

SPEED

1. In about three minutes fifty seconds (or about fifteen miles per hour—an unsustainable speed for humans). The four-minute mile was once thought unattainable but was achieved by Roger Bannister in 1954, since when it has been beaten many times.
2. About 186,000 miles a second. It is less in other media.
3. One nautical mile per hour (a nautical mile being 6,076.1 feet).
4. 25,000 miles per hour, or seven miles per second. From the moon's surface, the escape velocity is 1.5 miles per second.
5. 1,089 feet per second. Its speed increases by about two feet per second for every centigrade degree rise in temperature.
6. The cheetah sprints faster. It is the swiftest four-footed animal alive, able to run over short distances at sixty miles per hour. Thoroughbred horses, on the other hand, can gallop at forty-five miles per hour for a mile or more—so taking into consideration both speed and endurance, they are considered by some to be the fastest creatures in existence.
7. The penguin is faster: it can swim up to twenty-five miles per hour as it pursues squid, fish, or shrimp. A roadrunner runs at most up to fifteen miles per hour with its long tail extended horizontally, head down, and ragged crest erect.
8. They move at about the same speed. Sap rises at the rate of one to four feet per hour. Moles, which have extremely broad front feet with enormous digging claws, dig about twenty yards of tunnel a day.
9. The solar wind, at 450 miles per second, is considerably faster (and is even faster during periods of greater sunspot activity). By contrast, the Gulf Stream flows from the Gulf of Mexico north off the southeast coast of the United States into the Atlantic Ocean at a mere four miles per hour.
10. About four months. Nails consist of dead cells pushed outward by dividing cells in the root, a fold of epidermis at the base of the nail.

FREQUENCY

1. Every four years. The U.S. president can serve only two four-year terms. For Congress, members of the U.S. House of Representatives are elected every two years, and senators every six years.

2. Every year. The awards, first given in 1901, are for outstanding achievement in one of five fields: physics, chemistry, physiology or medicine, literature, peace. An award in economics was first given in 1969.

3. Every four years. They began, according to tradition, in Greece in 776 B.C., but were discontinued at the end of the fourth century A.D. The first modern Olympic games were held in Athens in 1896.

4. Every four years. In leap years there are 366 days instead of 365. Leap year originated with the Julian calendar of the Romans and was carried over during the gradual transition to the Gregorian calendar.

5. At rest, seventy-two times a minute (faster in physically active adults). In infants the rate may be as high as 120 beats per minute, and in children about 90 beats per minute.

6. The bat's soundings, sometimes as high as two hundred times a second, are much more frequent. The sounds echo from every object encountered, thus guiding the bat by providing information about the size, shape, and distance of each. Hummingbirds beat their wings from fifty to seventy-five times a second and must feed constantly to support the enormous amount of energy needed for this continuous movement.

7. Electrical current (sixty cycles per second in U.S. households), is more frequent. "Tommy guns" (Thompson submachine guns, developed in the 1920s) fire between seven and ten rounds of .45 caliber cartridges a second.

8. The earth and the moon revolve and rotate about their common center of mass at the same rate: once a month. It is the earth's gravitational influence on the moon that is responsible for this.

9. The earth rotates on its axis once a day (or, about every twenty-four hours). The sun rotates on its axis about once a month (or, more accurately, once every twenty-five days at its equator, and once every thirty-five days at its poles).

10. The earth revolves around the sun much more frequently—once a year. The sun revolves around the Milky Way once every two hundred million years (at a speed of about 155 miles per second).

TEMPERATURE

1. 212 degrees Fahrenheit or 100 degrees Celsius. Many English-speaking countries changed from the Fahrenheit to the Celsius scale in the 1960s and 1970s. A notable exception is the United States.
2. Subtract 32 degrees, then multiply the result by ⅚ (or by .555).
3. A fever would run above 98 degrees Fahrenheit (37 degrees Celsius), which is generally considered to be the normal body temperature.
4. Absolute zero is 0 degrees Kelvin (-273.16 degrees Celsius or -459.69 degrees Fahrenheit). This is the temperature at which the volume of an ideal gas would be zero and, theoretically, all molecular motion would cease. In actuality, all gases condense well above this point.
5. Add forty to the number of chirps per fifteen seconds, and you get a fair approximation of the temperature in degrees Fahrenheit.
6. Birds' body temperature, which is two to fourteen degrees Fahrenheit higher than that of mammals.
7. The moon's highest surface temperature is hotter—about 212 degrees Fahrenheit or 100 degrees Celsius, compared to the earth's highest recorded temperature of 136 degrees Fahrenheit (58 degrees Celsius). This was recorded at Azizia, Libya, in September 1922.
8. The oxyacetylene torch's flame: 6,300 degrees Fahrenheit (3,480 degrees Celsius). The torch can be used for cutting steel and welding iron, which melts at about 2,750 degrees Celsius.
9. The melting point of water (in the form of ice), which is 32 degrees Fahrenheit or 0 degrees Celsius. That of mercury is -38.87 degrees Celsius. Mercury is the only metal that exists as a liquid at temperatures that humans can tolerate.

10. The temperature at fusion, which is 50 million degrees Celsius for the fusion of deuterium with tritium and 400 million degrees Celsius for the fusion of tritium with tritium, is hotter. In this zone of high temperature all matter is vaporized at extremely high pressure, producing a huge destructive shock wave. The sun's temperature is 10 to 20 million degrees Celsius. The temperature of the bright surface of the sun is about 6,000 degrees Celsius.

WEIGHT

1. About two or three pounds (or, to be more exact, 2¼ to 3¼ pounds). Differences in size and weight do not signify corresponding differences in mental ability. The human liver weighs about the same as the brain.

2. From ten to sixteen pounds. Bowling balls have three or four finger holes, which help the bowler roll the balls down an alley at ten maple pins sixty feet away.

3. Exactly 2.205 avoirdupois pounds. The kilogram is defined in terms of a prototype cylinder kept in the International Bureau of Weights and Measures, established in 1875, at Sèvres, France.

4. From five hundred to six hundred pounds. Some Bactrian camels can carry as much as one thousand pounds. With these loads, camels can cover about thirty miles a day.

5. More than 3,000 tons. The spacecraft itself weighed forty-four tons. The assembly stood 363 feet high at launch.

6. They weigh about the same: about three pounds.

7. An elephant weighs more. Elephants weigh up to six to eight tons, whereas hippopotamuses weigh about five tons.

8. A human brain would weigh more. It weighs about three pounds, whereas a brontosaurus brain weighed about a pound. A brontosaurus's eyes and nostrils were on the top of its head, so it could see and breathe when it was almost totally submerged.

9. A blue whale would weigh more. Blue whales, the largest animals that have ever lived, weigh up to 120 tons. Brontosauruses weighed over thirty tons.

10. The Stonehenge stones are heavier. They weigh up to one hundred tons, whereas the Easter Island heads weigh about fifty tons. The heads range in height from ten to forty feet.

DISTANCE

1. Twenty-six miles. It is the distance from Marathon to Athens. Pheidippides ran the distance to bring the news of Athenian victory over the Persians at Marathon in 490 B.C. Today marathons are held every year in many U.S. cities, including New York and Boston.

2. Roughly 24,830 miles. As the earth is slightly flattened at the poles, its equatorial diameter is about twenty-six miles greater than its polar diameter.

3. About 200 miles (205 to be exact). Philadelphia lies between Washington and New York.

4. About 350 miles (347 to be exact). Both San Francisco and Los Angeles are large California cities and major seaports.

5. About 2,500 miles (2,451 to be exact). Flights from New York on the Atlantic coast to Los Angeles on the Pacific generally take passengers over the Middle Atlantic states, states of the Midwest, the Great Plains states, the Rocky Mountain states, and states of the Far West.

6. About fifty-five miles. The Bering Strait is between Alaska and Siberia.

7. About 240,000 miles, which is about ten times the journey around the earth at the equator.

8. About 93 million miles, which is about 387 times earth's distance from the moon.

9. 4.3 light-years (that is, it would take 4.3 years if you were traveling at the speed of light). The nearest star after the sun is Proxima Centauri, and it is nearly 26 million million miles away (or about 280,000 times the distance from the earth to the sun).

10. It would take about 2 million light-years to travel to our nearest neighbor, the Andromeda Galaxy, which is visible to the naked eye as a faint patch in the constellation Andromeda.

AREA

1. 5,333 square yards. (It is a rectangle 100 yards by 53 ⅓ yards.)
2. 4,840 square yards. (Imagine a rectangle 100 yards by about 50 yards—or slightly smaller than a football field.)
3. 18 acres. The attractive White House grounds have broad lawns, fountains, trees, and gardens.
4. There are 640 acres in a square mile, which is also equivalent to 2.59 square kilometers.
5. 840 acres. The largest park in New York City, Central Park occupies an area in the heart of midtown Manhattan, bounded by 59th Street on the south, Fifth Avenue on the east, 110th Street on the north, and Central Park West on the west.
6. Grenada. It covers 120 square miles, whereas Manhattan Island covers 22 square miles.
7. Texas. The state occupies 267,339 square miles and is larger than many European countries, including Spain, which occupies 194,884 square miles.
8. Iran (636,290 square miles) is five times the size of Iraq (167,924 square miles).
9. Canada is larger. It occupies 3,851,311 square miles, whereas the United States occupies 3,615,191 square miles (including Alaska and Hawaii).
10. The sea, by far. The interconnected mass of water covers 70.78 percent of the earth's surface.

NATURE

1. Six. Insects have three parts: a head, a thorax, and an abdomen. On their thorax they have three pairs of legs and two pairs of wings.
2. Eight. Spiders have a two-part body, with no wings.
3. Eight. One of the arms of the male octopus is modified into a sexual organ. Squids have ten arms.
4. Less than a hundred. On average, centipedes have 70 legs, although their name does mean "hundred-legged." However, some species do have as many as 360 legs.
5. Less than a thousand, although the name means "thousand-legged." Millipedes do, however, generally have far more

legs than centipedes, because they have two pairs of legs on each body segment except the first few and the last, whereas centipedes have only one pair on each segment.

6. Bacteria are microscopic one-celled organisms found in the bodies of all living creatures—including insects. There are, therefore, more bacteria (as separate creatures) than any other type of organism. There may be as many as 100 million bacteria in one gram of fertile soil.

7. The crocodile eggs are produced in the greater number, usually about twenty deposited in a nest of rotting vegetation and dug up when their mother hears them hatching. When kangaroos give birth, they produce only a single baby kangaroo.

8. It is the same number, about 30,000. The herring eggs are produced at one spawn, whereas the termite eggs are produced at the rate of 30,000 a day. Many species of fish produce as many as five million eggs in one spawn.

9. There are more lions. Lions are the only cats that are social rather than solitary, and they stay in groups (called prides) of up to thirty individuals. Tigers are solitary.

10. The Mexican freetail bats in Carlsbad Caverns can number as many as nine million. When these bats leave the caves together at dusk, it takes the entire column about twenty minutes to make its exit. Half a million penguins have been counted on a 500-acre colony in Antarctica.

THE UNIVERSE AND THE WORLD

1. There are fifty states, including Alaska and Hawaii. The federal District of Columbia and the present Commonwealth of Puerto Rico are two possible future prospects.

2. There are seven continents: Africa, Antarctica, Asia, Australia, Europe, North America, and South America.

3. The nine known planets are (from the sun outward): Mercury, Venus, Earth, Mars, Jupiter, Saturn, Uranus, Neptune, and Pluto.

4. Astronomers estimate there are about one hundred billion stars in the Milky Way. Our galaxy is shaped like a spiral disk, which we see edgewise (owing to our place in it). Its

glow is due to the combined light of the stars in the region of the plane of the disk.

5. Astronomers estimate that there are more galaxies in the universe than there are stars in our galaxy—in other words, over a hundred billion. A typical galaxy has a diameter of about 100,000 light-years.

6. At the North Pole. There are twenty-four sunlight hours there on midsummer day. At the equator on the same date, there are twelve.

7. There are far more languages in the world—between three and four thousand. The numbers of speakers of each language range from many millions down to a few dozen or even fewer. As of 1993, there were 109 chemical elements known.

8. There are more fern species. They number several thousand, whereas there is only *one* species of humankind—homo sapiens.

9. There are more species of birds, of which there are some 8,650, whereas there are about 6,000 reptile species.

10. There are more species of insects, of which there about 700,000. Thousands of new insect species are described each year. There are over 20,000 species of fish, which range in size from the $\frac{1}{2}$-inch goby of the Philippines to the 45-foot whale shark.

GROUPS AND GATHERINGS

1. Eleven players. Most organized football clubs have offensive and defensive squads, which alternate as possession of the ball changes.

2. Usually twelve, as in the movie *Twelve Angry Men*. Grand juries have from twelve to twenty-three members, petty (petit) juries twelve members.

3. Nine. The Court began in 1789 with six members and was increased to seven in 1807, to nine in 1837, and to ten in 1863. In 1866 the membership was reduced to eight to prevent President Andrew Johnson from filling any vacancies. Since 1869 the court has comprised nine members.

4. As of 1993, there were one hundred (two senators from each state). U.S. senators have six-year terms in office.

5. Six in 1993. They are the chairman; the vice chairman; the chief of staff, U.S. army; the chief of naval operations; the chief of staff, U.S. air force; and the marine corps commandant.

6. An American baseball team, which has nine players: a pitcher, a catcher, four infielders, and three outfielders. An American basketball team has five players.

7. The Houston Astrodome. Seating 60,000, the steel-supported structure was the first covered, temperature-controlled arena. The Roman Colosseum could accommodate about 45,000 spectators, who sat on marble seats.

8. Pilgrims to Mecca (as also to Lourdes, France) in a year number in the millions, whereas the runners in the New York City Marathon number in the thousands.

9. 25,000 tenants. The Empire State Building, built 1930–31, was for many years the tallest building in the world (102 stories).

10. Nearer twenty million people. *Reader's Digest*, established in 1922, has built its vast circulation with condensations of books and magazine articles.

POPULATION

1. Nearer one million. The population of Washington, D.C., was 606,900 in 1990. The Washington metropolitan area's population was 3,923,574.

2. Nearer seven million. New York City's population in 1990 was estimated to be 7,322,564. New York City is the largest city in the United States and one of the largest in the world. The population of the New York metropolitan area, which encompasses parts of southeast New York State, northeast New Jersey, and southeast Connecticut, was estimated at 18,087,251 in 1990.

3. Nearer two hundred fifty million. The population of the United States was estimated as 248,709,873 in 1990. More than 70 percent of the population is urban, and the great majority is of European descent.

4. Nearer one billion people. The 1991 estimated population of

China was 1,151,487,000. It is the most populous country in the world.

5. Nearer five billion. In 1991 the world's population was about 5.4 billion, having increased from less than 3.7 billion in 1970 and 2.5 billion in 1950.

6. Hawaii. Its estimated population in 1990 was 1,100,500, whereas Alaska's was 550,043 (although in land area it is the largest state in the Union).

7. California. It is the most populous state in the United States, with a population of 29,760,021 (as of 1990) compared to New York State's population of 17,990,455.

8. Europe. Its 1973 population was 640 million whereas that of the United States is 249 million (as of 1990).

9. African Americans. They make up about 12 percent of the population of the United States. Hispanics account for 9 percent and are the fastest-growing ethnic group in the country. Asian Americans are almost 3 percent of the population; and Native Americans, with a population under two million, are less than 1 percent.

10. Jews. Roughly 2.5 percent of Americans adhere to Judaism; under 2 percent of Americans are members of the Islamic faith.

THE HUMAN BODY

1. Twenty. We develop our milk teeth between our sixth and thirtieth months. At about age six, the permanent teeth start to come in, replacing the milk teeth.

2. Thirty-two. The last of these permanent teeth (the wisdom teeth) may not appear until the twenty-fifth year and in some people do not appear at all.

3. Six. The blood carries oxygen and nutrients to the body tissues and carries away carbon dioxide and other wastes.

4. Nearer one hundred: 206, to be exact. The bones are held together by flexible tissue consisting of cartilage and ligaments.

5. Forty-six. Potatoes have forty-eight chromosomes; Drosophila fruit flies have eight.

6. The hand, which has twenty-seven bones: eight in the wrist,

five in the palm, three in each finger, and two in the thumb. The foot has twenty-six bones.

7. **Eggs at birth.** There are about half a million immature eggs in a female infant's ovary at birth. Starting at puberty, eggs mature successively, and one breaks through the ovarian wall about every twenty-eight days.

8. There are more salivary glands (six, or three pairs). There are only four fundamental tastes that can be detected by our taste buds: sweet, sour, salt, and bitter.

9. There are more chambers of the heart (four), whereas there are only three types of muscle: striated, smooth, and cardiac.

10. Muscle tissue, of which about 80 percent is water. About 60 percent of red blood cells is water. About 92 percent of blood plasma is water, and over half of most other tissues is water.

PERIODS OF POWER

1. Nearly three years (from January 20, 1961 to November 22, 1963). Kennedy's term is often described as a thousand days (two years and 306 days).

2. Slightly more than one term. Lincoln (1809–65) began his first term as president on March 4, 1861 (one hundred years before Kennedy) and was shot and killed in Washington, D.C., on April 14, 1865 (a little over a month into his second term).

3. Twelve years. As head of the Conservative party, Thatcher (b. 1925) served as England's first woman prime minister from 1979 until 1991 when she was replaced by John Major, the Conservatives' new leader. She served longer than any other twentieth-century prime minister.

4. More than twenty-five years. Elizabeth (1533–1603) was queen of England for forty-five years (from 1558 until she died in 1603). Unmarried and childless, she was the last Tudor monarch, and succession passed peacefully to James VI of Scotland (son of Mary, Queen of Scots, Elizabeth's executed rival).

5. More than seventy years. Louis XIV (1638–1715) was king of France from 1643 (when he was five years old) until he died

in 1715. "The Sun King" was in effective control of government for fifty-four of those years (1661–1715).

6. Mao Zedong (1893–1976). This Chinese communist leader was founder and first chairman of the People's Republic of China in 1949, was replaced in 1959, but held power as party leader until his death.

7. Ayatollah Ruholla Khomeini (1900–89). Khomeini was seventy-nine when he returned from exile to become the ultimate authority in Iran after the deposition of the Shah in 1979. He retained power in the Islamic republic until his death.

8. Golda Meir (1898–1978). A key political figure even before the creation of the State of Israel in 1948, Meir was seventy-one when she became prime minister in 1969. She resigned in 1974.

9. Augustus (63 B.C.–A.D.14). When Julius Caesar was killed in 44 B.C., Augustus (then known as Octavian) became dominant in Rome. His reforms were prudent and far-reaching. He was responsible for Rome's return from a military dictatorship to a constitutional rule.

10. Ivan the Terrible. Ivan IV (1530–84) had himself crowned tsar in 1547 at age seventeen. Notorious for his cruelty, he married seven times, disposing of his wives by forcing them to take the veil or ordering their murder. Eisenstein's film was made between 1942 and 1946.

NUMBERS IN RELIGION AND MYTHOLOGY

1. Ten. According to the Bible, these commandments were given to Moses on Mount Sinai. They have a paramount place in the ethical systems of Judaism, Christianity, and Islam.

2. Three: the Father, the Son (incarnate as Jesus), and the Holy Ghost. The Trinity is considered by Christian teachers to be a mystery, so it is called a truth of revelation.

3. Twelve: Peter, Andrew, James the greater, John, Thomas, James the less, Jude, Philip, Bartholomew, Matthew, Simon, and Judas. The list of Twelve Disciples traditionally includes Judas and not Matthias, and the list of Twelve Apostles includes Matthias and not Judas.

4. Eight. Hanukkah came to be linked with a miraculous cruse of oil that burned for eight days, leading to the practice of lighting special Hanukkah candles, one the first evening, two the second, and so on. The eight-branched candlestand, or menorah, is a frequent symbol of Hanukkah.

5. Three: Clotho, who spun the web of life; Lachesis, who measured its length; and Atropos, who cut it.

6. The Four Stages are: Celibate student life; householdership; forest hermitage; and complete renunciation of all ties with society and pursuit of spiritual liberation.

7. The nine Muses are Calliope (epic poetry and eloquence); Euterpe (music and lyric poetry); Erato (love poetry); Polyhymnia (sacred poetry and oratory); Clio (history); Melpomene (tragedy); Thalia (comedy); Terpsichore (choral song and dance); and Urania (astronomy).

8. The Five Duties are: To say and believe at least once "There is no god but God and Muhammad is his prophet"; to pray five times a day; to give alms; to fast at Ramadan; and to go at least once to Mecca.

9. The Eight Paths can usually be summarized in these eight steps: right views; right resolve; right speech; right action; right livelihood; right effort; right mindfulness; and right concentration.

10. The Five Relations are: sovereign and subject; parent and child; elder and younger brother; husband and wife; and friend and friend.

DEATH TOLLS

1. At least six million. By the end of World War II, in Hitler's "final solution of the Jewish question," six million Jews had been systematically murdered.

2. In this shocking incident of the Vietnam War, U.S. soldiers massacred 347 unarmed men, women, and children in a small hamlet. A congressional investigation in 1969 led to the conviction of the unit's commander, Lt. William Calley.

3. About 205,000. On August 6, 1945, 130,000 people were killed, missing, or wounded at Hiroshima. Three days later 75,000 people were killed or wounded at Nagasaki.

4. Approximately 23,000 were killed or wounded at Antietam on September 17, 1862, the losses being about evenly divided between the sides. It is said to have been the bloodiest day of the Civil War.

5. Over 600,000. Photographs by Matthew B. Brady and others reveal some of the horror behind the statistics.

6. The number of British killed at Ypres was greater. Between July and November 1917, the British slowly advanced five miles at Passchendaele through mud and rain, at a cost of 300,000 lives. At the Battle of the Bulge during December 1944 and January 1945, the Allies lost 77,000 lives.

7. The flu epidemic. To compute the total losses caused by World War I is impossible, but ten million dead and 209 million wounded is a conservative estimate. Then at the very end of the war and immediately after it, more than 20 million died of influenza.

8. The Korean War. In that war over 54,000 Americans died and 103,000 were wounded, while North and South Korean casualties were each at least ten times as high. In the Vietnam War, U.S. casualties were more than 50,000 dead. South Vietnamese dead were estimated to be more than 400,000, and Vietcong and North Vietnamese at over 900,000 dead.

9. Those who died in the Warsaw ghetto are the greater number, by far. In 1942 there were half a million Jews crowded into the isolated and restricted ghetto by the Germans. When Soviet troops liberated Warsaw in January 1945, only about two hundred Jews remained (thousands were shipped to concentration camps, where they died). In contrast, three hundred victims were burned at the stake as heretics when Mary I ("Bloody Mary"; reigned 1553–58) attempted to restore Catholicism in England.

10. The number of crucifixions was greater. Six thousand slaves were crucified along the Capua-Rome highway (the Appian Way). Spartacus had been killed in a battle with Crassus in Lucania, and three thousand Roman prisoners had been found unharmed in his camp. At Masada, which fifteen thousand Roman troops took after a two-year siege, almost all the one thousand Jewish defenders killed themselves rather than be enslaved. Two women and five children survived.

AGE AND ACHIEVEMENT

1. **In his forties.** When John Fitzgerald Kennedy (1917–63) defeated Richard Nixon in the 1960 election at the age of forty-three, he was the youngest man to be elected president.
2. **In his twenties.** John Keats (1795–1821) was one of the greatest English Romantic poets when he developed tuberculosis. He went to Italy, where he died at age twenty-five; he is buried in Rome.
3. **In her teens.** Anne Frank (1929–45) hid with her family for three years (1942–44) in a sealed-off room in an Amsterdam warehouse. During those years, Anne kept a diary marked by poignancy, insight, humor, and touching naïveté. The family was betrayed to the Germans in 1944.
4. **In his twenties.** Pablo Picasso (1881–1973) was well advanced in his long career as a painter when he painted his "blue period" work *The Old Guitarist* in 1903, but he was only twenty-two at the time.
5. **In his twenties.** Albert Einstein (1879–1955) was twenty-six when he formulated the special theory of relativity in 1905. He formulated the general theory of relativity in 1915, when he was thirty-seven.
6. **William Gates III (b. 1955).** He founded Microsoft in 1974 with Paul Allen. In 1992 Gates was listed as the richest man in the United States.
7. **Henri Matisse (1869–1954).** One of the original Fauves in his early years, the French painter, sculptor, and lithographer did his cutouts in his last years. He produced *Jazz* in 1947.
8. **Theodore Roosevelt (1858–1919).** At forty-two he was the youngest president in U.S. history. His championship in office of the rights of the "little man" captured the people's imagination, and in 1904 he was reelected in a landslide.
9. **Bertrand Russell (1872–1970).** The British philosopher had previously been imprisoned for pacifism in 1918, at age forty-six. He received the Nobel Prize for Literature in 1950.
10. **Barbara McClintock (1902–92).** The American geneticist discovered that certain genetic material provided a key for understanding cell differentiation. At first ignored, her work was later recognized as a major contribution to DNA research, and she was awarded the Nobel Prize in 1983.

HOW THEY DIED

1. He was crucified in A.D. 33. Jesus was convicted of blasphemy by Pontius Pilate, the Roman governor of Judaea, at the urging of the Jewish authorities.
2. He was given poisonous hemlock to drink. Socrates (469–399 B.C.), the Athenian philosopher, was convicted of corrupting youth and of religious heresies. His trial and death are described in three works by Plato with great dramatic power.
3. She was burned at the stake. In May 1429, during the Hundred Years' War, Joan of Arc (1412?–31) defeated the English. Two years later French clerics tried her for heresy because she claimed direct inspiration from God. She recanted, but later retracted her recantation.
4. He was beheaded. In 1649 Charles (1600–49) was tried by a high court controlled by his enemies and convicted of treason.
5. He was guillotined. Louis (1754–93) was tried by the French revolutionary Convention and condemned to death by a majority of one. He was guillotined in 1793.
6. Steve Biko (1946–77). His death prompted international protests and a UN arms embargo against South Africa.
7. Robert Kennedy (1925–68), younger brother of John F. Kennedy, was a senator from New York and a presidential candidate when he was assassinated. The gunman Sirhan Sirhan was captured and convicted of first-degree murder.
8. Anne Boleyn (1507?–36). Henry was bitterly disappointed that Anne's child was a daughter (later Elizabeth I), and soon took up with Jane Seymour. Whether Anne was guilty of adultery and incest has never been determined.
9. Crazy Horse. After Little Bighorn, Crazy Horse's camp was attacked, and he spent the winter with his one thousand followers in a state of near starvation. The group surrendered at the Red Cloud agency in May 1877.
10. Nat Turner (1800–31). The Southampton Insurrection, in which fifty-five whites were killed, was by far the most serious uprising in the history of slavery in the United States. The revolt was soon crushed, and thirteen slaves and three free blacks were hanged immediately. Turner escaped to the woods, but was captured six weeks later and hanged.

MONEY-MAKERS

1. From explosives. In 1866 Alfred Bernhard Nobel (1833–96), the Swedish chemist and inventor, perfected dynamite. He left a fund from the interest of which the international Nobel Prizes are given annually.
2. From shipping. In the 1940s Aristotle Socrates Onassis (1906?–75), his father-in-law Stavros Livanos, and his brother-in-law Stavros Niarchos, formed the most powerful shipping clan in the world. In 1968 Onassis married Jacqueline Bouvier Kennedy, widow of President John F. Kennedy.
3. From banking, shipbuilding, investment banking, and motion-picture distribution. Joseph Patrick Kennedy (1888–1969) was U.S. ambassador to Great Britain (1937–40), opposing American intervention in the Second World War. He was the father of John F. Kennedy, Robert F. Kennedy, and Edward M. Kennedy.
4. From trade and banking. The Medici family produced three popes, two queens of France, and several cardinals. They made Renaissance Florence the richest European cultural center since the Athens of Pericles.
5. From steel. Andrew Carnegie (1835–1919) sold his business to U.S. Steel in 1901 for $250 million in bonds. His benefactions totaled about $350 million, including Carnegie Hall (1892) and many other institutions.
6. Cornelius Vanderbilt (1794–1877). The family fortune has benefited not only Vanderbilt University but the College of Physicians and Surgeons, now part of Columbia University, and Teachers College, Columbia University.
7. The Rothschilds. This great family, springing from Mayer Amschel Rothschild (1743–1812), who was the son of a money changer in the Jewish ghetto of Frankfurt, Germany, was undoubtedly one of the world's chief financial powers in the nineteenth century.
8. John Pierpont Morgan (1837–1913). In 1901 he founded U.S. Steel Corp., the first billion-dollar corporation in the world. His name is commemorated not only in various financial institutions but in a wing of the Metropolitan Museum of Art in New York and at the Pierpont Morgan Library, also in New York.

9. Henry Clay Frick (1849–1919). His mansion in New York City, together with his art collection and an endowment of $15 million, was willed to the public as a museum.

10. Michael R. Milken (b. 1946). He became known as the "junk bond king." In 1990 he was sentenced to a ten-year prison term for violating U.S. securities and tax laws. In 1991 his sentence was reduced to two years in prison and three years of community service.